# LIBRARY OF HEBREW BIBLE/ OLD TESTAMENT STUDIES

# 445

*Formerly Journal for the Study of the Old Testament Supplement Series*

# BIBLICAL CORPORA

## Representations of Disability
## in Hebrew Biblical Literature

Rebecca Raphael

t&t clark

NEW YORK • LONDON

T & T Clark International, 80 Maiden Lane, New York, NY 10038

T & T Clark International, The Tower Building, 11 York Road, London SE1 7NX

T & T Clark International is a Continuum imprint.


Visit the T & T Clark blog at www.tandtclarkblog.com



**Library of Congress Cataloging-in-Publication Data**
A catalogue record for this book is available from the Library of Congress

|  |  |
|---|---|
| ISBN-10 | 056702802X |
| ISBN-13 | 9780567028020 |


06 07 08 09 10      10 9 8 7 6 5 4 3 2 1

*For John J. Collins, with gratitude.*
καὶ ἐδικαιώθη ἡ σοφία ἀπὸ πάντων τῶν τέκνων αὐτῆς

# CONTENTS

# ACKNOWLEDGMENTS

For this book, I own thanks to several colleagues in Texas. In Spring 2002, Aaron Bar-Adon allowed me to sit in on his Job seminar at the University of Texas at Austin. There, I scribbled the concept of what became the Job portion of this book on a handwritten translation of the divine speeches. The Southwestern Commission for the Study of Religion later accepted a paper proposal based on that idea, which I presented in Spring 2003. Kelley Coblentz-Bautch presided at that session and urged me immediately to pursue the idea. One week after that meeting, Mikeal Parsons of Baylor University emailed me an offer to consider the Job paper for publication in his journal, *Perspectives in Religious Studies*. That project became "Things Too Wonderful: A Disabled Reading of Job" (*Perspectives in Religious Studies* 31, no. 4 [2004]: 399–424). I thank Professor Parsons for the permission to incorporate large portions of that work here. I am indebted to him not only for publishing something that I did not think others would be interested in, but also for providing professional support in other ways to my work and to the development of disability studies within biblical studies.

Several scholars associated with what we called, during its inaugural term of 2004–2006, the Society of Biblical Literature Consultation on Biblical Scholarship and Disabilities have provided encouragement and responses to portions of this manuscript. Hector Avalos served as respondent at the 2003 American Academy of Religion session where I presented "Images of Disability in Hebrew Prophetic Literature," now the basis of part of Chapter 4. A month in advance of that AAR meeting, David Tabb Stewart, both a Texas and Disability Unit colleague, selected this paper for our local group, the Central Texas Biblical Studies Seminar of Austin and its environs. The discussions at both meetings steered the prophecy portion to much greater clarity. Again in 2006, Avalos responded to "Objects that Neither See Nor Hear: The Normate Construction of Divinity in Deuteronomic Literature" at the SBL International Meeting in Edinburgh. Rachel Magdalene and Kerry Wynn both engaged me in informal conversation about my various papers, in addition to contributing to the *Perspectives in Religious Studies* topical volume on disability, which Mikeal Parsons had invited me to guest edit

(*Perspectives in Religious Studies*, vol. 32, no. 1 [2007]). Finally, Jeremy Schipper responded to the penultimate draft of the Introduction, helpfully and on short notice. Beyond the scope of our unit, I presented "Evoked Potential: Representations of the Body in the Psalms" both to the Central Texas Biblical Studies Association and to the SBL Psalms unit in fall 2004. Both groups gave productive responses to my ideas on disability in the Psalms.

In addition to responding to my work in its early stages, two colleagues were generous in sharing theirs at pre-publication phases. I attended the 2004 inaugural session of the SBL Disability Unit, at which Hector Avalos presented his paper on sensory criticism. He later allowed me to have a version intermediate between that one and the article that appeared in the 2007 Semeia volume, *This Abled Body: Rethinking Disabilities in Biblical Studies* (Atlanta: SBL, 2007). David Tabb Stewart also gave me, on my request immediately following a 2005 SBL session, a copy of his paper "Deaf and Blind in Leviticus 19:14 and the Emergence of Disability Law." It proved insightful and helped clarify my thought on that material. And again, Jeremy Schipper sent me large portions of his dissertation, which soon became an installment in this LHBOTS series, *Disability Studies and the Hebrew Bible: Figuring Mephibosheth in the David Story* (New York: T&T Clark International, 2006). He kindly sent me the page proofs when I needed to write about them, but before the book was in print. Saul Olyan's book on disability in the Hebrew Bible came into print too late for me to include discussion of it in this work, although I was able to attend his presentation on prophecy and disability at the 2007 SBL meeting.

I also thank several people at Continuum for their indispensable role in bringing this project to print. Claudia Camp and Andrew Mein took a risk that they probably did not intend in accepting this manuscript on the basis of the proposal and several of the papers. Initially I worked with acquisitions editor Henry Carrigan, and then, when he moved on, with Burke Gerstenschlager. Both have been patient with some rather unusual life disruptions that delayed my completion of this manuscript. Thanks are also due to Duncan Burns of Forthcoming Publications, who provided indexing and made copyediting pleasant.

Finally, I owe a debt of a different kind to John J. Collins, with whom I worked as a graduate student at Chicago. He kindly read and critiqued the Edinburgh version of the Deuteronomy portion, and offered early encouragement for me to pursue this new subfield within biblical studies. That sort of help, although invaluable, is the least of it. Without him, I would not be working in biblical studies. I do not know whether that is good or bad for others, or for the field, but it is the truth.

# ABBREVIATIONS

| | |
|---|---|
| AAR | American Academy of Religion |
| *ABD* | *Anchor Bible Dictionary.* Edited by D. N. Freedman. 6 vols. New York, 1992 |
| ADA | Americans with Disabilities Act |
| *ANET* | *Ancient Near Eastern Texts Relating to the Old Testament.* Edited by J. B. Pritchard. 3d ed. Princeton, 1969 |
| *BHS* | *Biblia Hebraica Stuttgartensia* |
| DtH | The Deuteronomistic History |
| *JBL* | *Journal of Biblical Literature* |
| JPS | Jewish Publication Society |
| *JSSR* | *Journal for the Scientific Study of Religion* |
| KJV | King James (Authorized) Version |
| MT | Masoretic Text |
| NRSV | New Revised Standard Version |
| SBL | Society of Biblical Literature |
| *TAB* | *This Abled Body: Rethinking Disabilities in Biblical Studies.* Edited by Hector Avalos, Sarah J. Melcher, and Jeremy Schipper. Semeia Studies 55. Society of Biblical Literature, 2007 |

Chapter 1

## INTRODUCTION:
## DISABILITY STUDIES WITHIN BIBLICAL STUDIES

…But if horses or oxen or lions had hands or could draw with their hands
and accomplish such works as men, horses would draw the figures of the
gods as similar to horses, and the oxen as similar to oxen, and they would
make the bodies of the sort which each of them had.

—Xenophanes of Colophon[1]

Their idols are silver and gold, the work of human hands. They have
mouths, but do not speak; eyes, but do not see. They have ears, but do not
hear; noses, but do not smell. They have hands, but do not feel; feet, but
do not walk; they make no sound in their throats. Those who make them
are like them; so are all who trust in them.

—Ps 115:4–8[2]

This monograph employs the primarily literary methods of disability
studies to analyze the representation of disability in the Hebrew Bible.
This work is neither an historical-critical inventory of all passages
related to disability, nor a postmodern counter-reading in the service of
polemics or theology. Rather, it attempts to examine the systematic ways
that the Hebrew Bible represents disability and relates disability to its
other concepts. In the interest of sustained literary analysis, I focus on
single canonical books, or substantial portions thereof. Treating references to disability in isolation too easily contributes to the misconception
that disability plays a peripheral role. Such a strategy also often fails to
capture the long arc of representations within a given text. Conversely, in

---

1. *Xenophanes of Colophon: Fragments. A Text and Translation with a Commentary by J. H. Lesher* (Toronto: University of Toronto Press, 1992), 25.
2. Unless noted otherwise, biblical quotations are from the NRSV. Throughout, I
do occasionally use other or my own translations, if the NRSV proved unsuitable for
some point.

the interest of advancing a comprehensive thesis, I selected representative texts from each major genre of Hebrew biblical literature—law, narrative, wisdom, poetry, and prophecy. Some selections have trans- or inter-generic features.

As a cultural text of singular potency in Western, and now global, civilization, the Bible has deeply informed representations, attitudes, and practices concerning disability in any given post-biblical world. If one reflects casually on its influence, proof-texting scraps will probably come to mind first: Isaac's blind providential gesture, Jacob's blessed limp, Jesus' healing of the mute demoniacs who nevertheless refuse, or are not allowed, to speak post-operatively, as it were.[3] Neither Jewish nor Christian Bibles speak with one voice here. If one wants to wax homiletic, with or without benefit of clergy, the stock of prooftexts offers ample supplies both for comforting my people and for condemning them. Selective readings, in either direction, depend on isolating the passages, and thus isolating biblical disability, just as social practices isolate disabled persons. Use of the Bible's generic passages of universal equity and inclusion to paint a highly favorable picture of disability fails to ask whether the more general concepts—God's power, for instance—depend in any important way on the always complex and often negative representation of disability. Alternatively, one might deplore the backward attitudes, if one feels inclined to smugness about the bodily regulations of Leviticus, and hold the text up for politically correct ridicule. But all of these strategies of popular and scholarly biblical interpretation avoid the question of what, if anything, the profluent disability imagery has to do with the Bible's major categories: holiness, ethics, historiography, exile, prophecy, wisdom, God.

Presumption should favor the working hypothesis that the frequent use of disability terms and images suggests that biblical representations of disability are integrally related to other biblical categories, not tacked on like a prosthetic attached to a body that has all of its limbs. This is not to say that we can expect a high degree of coherence of the sort that yields a consistent valuation, that is, either disabled persons are specially protected by God and ought to be so by humankind, or that they are specially indicative of evil, their own or others'. They may not be special at all, just part of the whole picture, in dynamic relation to other parts. Questions of consistency and significance in the biblical representations of disability cannot be addressed until we survey those representations as a whole and look for their connections to other biblical categories. I

---

3.   Gen 27; 32; Matt 9; 12.

would compare the case to feminist hermeneutics in this respect: isolation with an interest in valuation will fail to ask about the big picture, and so fail to find it, if there is one. For instance, one could isolate the Woman of Valor poem in Prov 31, and interpret it as a positive image of a strong woman, so successful that her husband can spend his days in leisurely discussion with other men. Or one could elevate the household codes in the Pseudo-Pauline epistles, point to a clearly subordinate role for women, and think that is either abhorrent or God's plan. Deeper feminist hermeneutics asks instead, "How male is this God? Who made him male? And what follows? Where is the female to be found, and what is she doing?" Likewise with disability: in order to discover deep structures of abled and disabled categories, we must survey a range of biblical material and investigate connections, both among the representations of disability, and across other categories such as power, election, and holiness.

To be sure, historical reconstruction provides a necessary grounding and context for representational analysis. We can expect some historical layering in how disability is represented and what it signifies in different strata. We should not assume a highly consistent picture in the composite text; in fact, the Hebrew Bible represents disability in variegated ways. Exploration of this variety must precede generalizations about disability's intersection with other categories of biblical thought. Finally, after careful examination of the variety, I shall step back and view the repertoire of canonical representations, not because I believe that the canonical form has privileged metaphysical authority (I do not), but because it empirically has privileged cultural authority.

This introduction has three main objectives. First, I shall discuss the major contributions of the new subfield of disability studies. Since it emerged in literary criticism within the United States and in social science in the United Kingdom, disability studies is not yet well known to most biblical scholars. This situation, however, is changing rapidly. The second major purpose of the introduction is a survey of recent work at the intersection of biblical studies and disability studies. Finally, I shall discuss the more general intellectual commitments and approaches to biblical scholarship that inform my analysis of disability in the Hebrew Bible.

As a foreshadowing of those commitments, consider the Xenophanes epigram above. This well-known quip about divine anthropomorphism touches on deeper problems than it addresses explicitly. Consider a horse (assisted, perhaps, by a prosthetic attachment that could hold a paint brush) painting the god of horses. What kind of horse will the horse-artist paint? Stallion or mare? What breed and coat color? War horse or work horse, race horse or show? A wild horse, and if so, is wildness deep as an unconscious assumption, or does it contrast with another state? Would it be a foal or an aged horse with cataracts and arthritis? Will there be a lame horse, for instance—a horsy equivalent of Hephaistos? A polytheist horse society might have such a figure, but is it likely if horses are monotheists? Would it matter greatly if the god of horses were represented in visual or verbal art? If this example seems silly, here is my serious point: any representation, visual or linguistic, of a deity must select elements for the representation. Those selected elements either are, or will become, more closely associated with divinity; this implies that some aspects of horse nature are more god-like and others less or not at all. But what is the prior index of god-likeness that guides the selection? Xenophanes hit the species-centric nail on the head, but gods are not represented as just any member of a species. Religious authorities, artists, and authors, compose gods from what they value most about human experience. Every god encodes a valuation, even a sacralization, of certain human traits. The body is prominent among these traits, which also include cognitive and emotional traits. It should go without saying but does not: bodies also have bodily traits.

Is the God of the Hebrew Bible different? I think not. In spite of the prohibitions against images, the Bible contains copious verbal imagery of God. The Hebrew difference moves away from the concreteness of polytheistic iconography, but it does not and cannot fly free of human imagination. The Hebrews imagined their God in terms of the human body: he has at least one hand (Isa 5:25; Pss 44:2–3; 98:1, etc.); superlatively powerful vision and hearing (Ps 145:19–20; Exod 2:24; Deut 5:28, etc.); and male gender (every pronoun and virtually all humanoid images), among other things. The Hebrew Bible also sacralizes the human body, or at least certain variations of it. God demands that human beings, or at least some of them, move, see, and hear in some ways and not in others. Even in such an anti-iconic tradition, requirements addressed to the human body nevertheless express concepts about God. That is, the human body provides an indirect representation of the divine (Gen 1:26–27). It is unfortunate to disembody the Genesis passage and turn it into an anthropopathism or an anthropocognitive faculty, for the passage itself juxtaposes "image of God" with "male and female," a very embodied illustration of the concept. Indeed, divine representations that avoided all reference to human bodies would seem to lack substance, even for the mind. Sometimes the representation is straightforward, as in the Levitical representation of priestly, unblemished, male bodies as better agents or images of holiness than other kinds of bodies. Sometimes the human represents the divine by reversal, as when an infertile woman conceives by divine agency. I could multiply variations, but suffice it to say that representations of human bodies and of God subsist within the same system of representations and are deeply implicated in each other.

## What is Disability Studies?

One must first ask, what is disability? As a term, "disability" currently holds the neutral ground, in contrast to other terms that have fallen out of favor, for example, "handicapped" (passé), "crippled" (derogatory), "invalid" (patently offensive). However humane or polite the term, the basic idea seems to be that a body part, sense, or function is not present or does not perform according to standard specs. This common-sense notion is fraught with difficulty. Human bodies show a wide range of anatomical, physiological, and functional variety. Which variations count as disabilities? The Americans with Disabilities Act of 1990 defined the concept thus: "Disability—The term 'disability' means, with respect to an individual—(A) a physical or mental impairment that substantially limits one or more of the major life activities of such individual; (B) a record of such an impairment; (C) being regarded as having such an impairment."[4] United States Federal law thus distinguishes between variations with negligible effect on life activities and those which significantly alter life functions. The variation known as color blindness, for instance, could be understood as the lack of some feature expected to be present, but it does not limit one's life in the ways that paraplegia does, at least not in our society. Life-activity impairment is a spectrum, not one part of a dichotomy. A further difficulty lies in the complicated interaction of disabled bodies with social environments. In the nearly-universal experience of people with disabilities, the physical condition in itself can be distinguished from barriers added to it by social attitudes and by exclusionary practices. Consider, for instance, the person who uses a wheelchair. Before ramps and accessible restroom stalls were common, many people remained at home. To the able-bodied, this extremely restricted mobility seemed to be an unfortunate result of not being ambulatory. Actually it is a result of buildings not having ramps and appropriate restroom facilities. Some disabled persons will be familiar with the disability multiplier effect, as when a speaker assumes that a wheelchair-user is also deaf. (I know of a deaf woman who was asked whether she

4. Americans with Disabilities Act of 1990, S. 933, section 3, paragraph 2. Online: http://caselaw.lp.findlaw.com/casecode/uscodes/42/chapters/126/toc.html (accessed September 22, 2008).

could drive a car.) Defining disability, even by itself, is difficult. Separating the mixture of bodily (dis)abilities and social barriers that could be different requires great discernment. Yet these distinctions place great attention on disability as the term needing definition. But what is "normal"? That question is just as difficult.[5]

As an emerging field of social science and humanities, disability studies has grappled with definitional terms and models. A scholarly consensus has emerged around a recent historical shift in how disability is characterized.[6] We speak of models, that is, conceptual schemes, for understanding disability. The early modern medical model equates disability with bodily impairment, and tries to cure individuals, by analogy with disease. This model remains powerful enough that the reader may wonder how else disability can be understood. Let us consider the unstated assumptions behind the medical model. First, the model locates disability entirely in the individual's body. Thus the burden of negotiating the world falls entirely on the individual. Given the exclusive focus on physical impairment, the medical model calls for cures. Since the medical model treats disabled people as sick people, it leads to practical actions that treat disabled people like sick people. Just as the sick are isolated in special institutions run by medical authorities, so the disabled were isolated in special institutions run by medical authorities. Most important, the medical model obscures the significant role that social practices play in amplifying the consequences of impairments. When a society looks only for cures, it may overlook its practices about architecture, media, and public services. In effect, the medical model, whatever its benefits, too easily absolves society for refusing to include its disabled persons by failing to change things that really do lie within human power to change.

In an early conceptual move beyond the medical model, scholars and disability rights activists proposed a distinction between impairment and disability. Impairment is just physical: some organ does not perform properly, or some biochemical pathway does not function. The physical condition would be present, regardless of the bearer's environment. Disability, on the other hand, refers to the result of a misfit between physical impairment and social environment. A blind person becomes

5. Lennard Davis, *Enforcing Normalcy: Disability, Deafness, and the Body* (London: Verso, 1995), 2.

6. For a philosophical appraisal of various ways of conceiving disability, see Anita Silvers, "Formal Justice," in *Disability, Difference, Discrimination: Perspectives on Justice in Bioethics and Public Policy* (New York: Rowman & Littlefield, 1998), 13–145.

more disabled in a social world that requires use of a car, than he or she was in a pre-automotive village. The body has not changed, but the social environment has. Impairment becomes disability because of the ways society chooses to build its spaces and communicate its information. This distinction between impairment and disability arises from both observable historical changes in what impairments are disabling and to what extent, and also from the lived experience of people with disabilities.

While this distinction usefully directs attention to how social practices work with or against a given bodily variation, it has been challenged. The point at which an impairment becomes a disability can be quite murky. If someone has a visual impairment that can be corrected with glasses, we do not call her disabled. Suppose the condition progresses. When she can longer drive at night, is she disabled? Perhaps not. However, when she can no longer drive at all, most inhabitants of post-industrial societies would now regard her condition as a disability. Is it biological or social that we need to operate during the day more so than at night? At what exact moment did the impairment become a disability? Literary critic Lennard Davis has played a major role in breaking down the identity problems that emerge from a too-rigid distinction between impairment and disability.[7] Nevertheless, I believe the distinction proves useful in locating the bodily versus social dimensions of a situation, and will employ it without over-stating it as a categorical distinction.

In the wake of critique of the medical model, several other models have been proposed. The social model made significant use of the impairment–disability distinction, to the extent of identifying disability almost entirely as a social construction.[8] Drawing on theories of oppression, this model views disabled persons as a minority oppressed by a majority; physical difference provides the pretext, but the oppression serves a hegemonic strategy. This model can perhaps be best understood by analogy to sexism and racism. Feminist critics have long pointed out the absurdity of taking only half of the human species as a norm and treating the other as divergent or "abnormal." In the case of biological sex, our traditional concept of "norm" is obviously not statistical but ideological. To say that does not deny the biological reality of different

7. Lennard Davis, *Bending Over Backwards: Disability, Dismodernism, and Other Difficult Positions* (New York: New York University Press, 2002), Chapter 1, "The End of Identity Politics and the Beginning of Dismodernism: On Disability as an Unstable Category."

8. Jeremy Schipper, *Disability Studies and the Hebrew Bible: Figuring Mephibosheth in the David Story* (New York: T&T Clark International, 2006), 16–18.

sexes; it merely points out that ideology, not biology, marks one sex as the norm and the other as inferior relative to that norm. Similarly, a real physical difference, namely variation in the amount and types of melanin in the skin, would hardly be enough to support an entire racist system. Many further attributions occur, and many systemic practices contribute to the construction of "race." Again, such strategies seem to have little to do with a statistical norm: most human beings today are not "white," and yet within a white racist ideology, "white" constitutes the "real" human-ity from which the other diverges. With disability, the numbers vary: global estimates from the 1980s put the incidence of disability at 10%.[9] While not a majority or half of a 50–50 split, disabled persons are hardly rare. Yet their exclusion from social status occurs disproportionately to their numbers.[10] Like the medical model, the social model implies a course of action: agitation for civil rights, public services, and the option for inclusion.[11] In the case of the Deaf community, for instance, this model fits well with the community's self-understanding as a minority linguistic community with a common history and culture.

Disability scholars in humanities have integrated the advantages of various models into what biblical scholar Jeremy Schipper, following dialogue with David T. Mitchell, calls "the cultural model."[12] Although it emerged in the 1990s in response to the inadequacies of the social model, the mid-century sociologist Erving Goffman hit upon some of its key insights. His 1963 book *Stigma: Notes on the Management of Spoiled Identity* broke new conceptual ground, for it examined disability as a social-relational phenomenon that included the able-bodied as a crucial

---

9.  Davis, *Normalcy*, 7.

10.  The following statistics are from Andrew J. Houtenville, "Disability Statis-tics in the United States," Ithaca, NY: Cornell University Rehabilitation Research and Training Center. Online: www.disabilitystatistics.org. Posted May 15, 2003 (accessed June 13, 2008). The percentage of people seeking employment but not employed is 4.6 among the non-disabled, and 6.3 among the disabled; not actively seeking employment and not employed, 18.2 % among non-disabled, 55.7% among disabled (employment figures for 2005); among men and women aged 21–64, the poverty rate among those without an impairment that affected work was 8.9%, but 28.2% among those with an impairment that affected work (figures from 2004).

11.  Inclusion can be difficult to define. For instance, many Deaf activists regard mainstreaming as a form of exclusion because it isolates the Deaf student in an environment that is likely to be disadvantageous, whereas Deaf schools where American Sign Language is the language of instruction and student culture would be inclusive.

12.  Schipper, *Mephibosheth*, 16. Mitchell's work will be discussed in detail below.

part of the dynamic. Goffman saw stigma as a necessary corollary of social norms: "It is not to the different that one should look for understanding our differentness, but to the ordinary. The question of social norms is certainly central, but the concern might be less for uncommon deviations from the ordinary than for ordinary deviations from the common."[13] Not only does a given society construct norm and difference, but it also prescribes the manner of being different: whether or not to show shame, whether or not to pass, whether to minimize or maximize the difference, and so on. Goffman concluded, "...the role of normal and the role of stigmatized are parts of the same complex, cut from the same cloth."[14] This key observation that disability (and for Goffman, other types of "spoiled" identities) is a property of social relations and not just bodies became a major point of departure for disability studies.

Literary critics working three decades later took the idea of a "normal"– "spoiled" duet into historical and literary analysis. Using lexical and historical evidence, Lennard Davis points out that the concept of a norm arises in the context of modern industrial societies.[15] Ancient societies— by which he means Greco-Roman cultures—postulated an ideal body type that no real body could achieve. For this ideal–real binary, modernity substituted a "real" norm for which disability was the necessary opposite: "The concept of the norm, unlike that of an ideal, implies that the majority of the population must or should somehow be part of the norm... With the concept of the norm comes the concept of deviations or extremes."[16] Rosemarie Garland Thomson, a critic of nineteenth-century American literature, coined the term *normate* for this ideological "norm":

> The term normate usefully designates the social figure through which people can represent themselves as definitive human beings. Normate, then, is the constructed identity of those who, by way of the bodily configurations and cultural capital they assume, can step into a position of authority and wield the power it grants them.[17]

If the jargon is unfortunate, the need for it is real: even among scholars, many are situated so deeply in this cultural self that they cannot grasp the difference between a biological fact and a social construction. Once,

13. Erving Goffman, *Stigma: Notes on the Management of Spoiled Identity* (New York: Simon & Schuster, 1963), 127.
14. Ibid., 130.
15. Davis, *Normalcy*, 24.
16. Ibid., 29.
17. Rosemarie Garland Thomson, *Extraordinary Bodies: Figuring Physical Disability in American Culture and Literature* (New York: Columbia University Press, 1997), 8.

when presenting a portion of this book as a paper to a group of colleagues,[18] I attempted to point out the ideology behind prophetic passages that employ "cures" of disabled persons as signs of the prophetic *eschaton* in Isaiah. One colleague in the audience protested several times that "they are still handicapped"—meaning that "they" really did signify something wrong with the cosmos that God would of course put right, and was I suggesting that God just leave "them" that way? Yet there are, after all, many steps and structures, unconscious though they may be, from the "real" impaired body to the body as sign of the *eschaton*, or of anything else. Given the infelicitous quality of "normate," I shall simply used a capitalized Normal to refer to the ideological "right" body.

Regarding the mixture of factual bodies and ideologies, David T. Mitchell and Sharon L. Snyder note that attributions of physical, cognitive, or emotional deficits have been used to construct inferior categories (female, colored, queer), and that one response to such oppression is to deny that these attributions are "real." For example, sexist ideology categorized women as intellectually inferior to men, and sexist practice proscribed female participation in math, science, and humane scholarship.[19] One standard feminist reply has been to assert that women do not really have the attributed cognitive deficits. But what of people who do?

Mitchell and Snyder point out that this move leaves actual impairment as the substratum of "reality" that *would* justify assigned inferiority. They conclude: "…disability occupies a unique identity that must navigate the terrain between physical/cognitive differences and social stigma. No purely constructivist reading can adequately traverse this political and experiential divide."[20] This is so because the different body "really" is different in ways that lie outside of and precede ideology. And yet: "One might think of disability as the master trope of human disqualification."[21] This is empirically true, for a discourse of disability has historically been used to define inferior categories and to justify oppression of persons who fall into the category. To return to the distinction between impairment and disability, one might ask what exactly makes *this* bodily difference have *all* the social implications that it does.

---

18. Rebecca Raphael, "Images of Disability in Hebrew Prophetic Literature" (paper presented to the Central Texas Biblical Studies Seminar, Austin, October 24, 2003).

19. David T. Mitchell and Sharon L. Snyder, *Narrative Prosthesis: Disability and the Dependencies of Discourse* (Ann Arbor: The University of Michigan Press, 2000), 3.

20. Ibid.

21. Ibid.

In short, while acknowledging the existence of real physical differences, Davis, Garland Thomson, and Mitchell and Snyder all treat disability as part of larger representational systems and ideological structures. One cannot begin to define disability without reference to something else, and that something else also requires definition. Schipper summarizes this model and its implications thus:

> ...according to the cultural model, disability is not only a result of social organization, but integral to social organization itself. Thus, the goal of disability studies becomes not jus the isolation and removal of social barriers that disabled people with impairments, but the interrogation of how society uses the category "disability" to narrate, interpret, and organize its world. In this sense, representations of disability are not value-free or transparent, but help to develop and work out social and cultural ideologies or worldviews.[22]

To transpose this description into historical terms, disability studies seeks to elucidate the role of disability within the overall thought structure and value system of a given set of texts or artifacts, from a given time and place.

Mitchell and Snyder provide a useful typology of disability studies.[23] In surveying the field in 2000, they list five major approaches. First, studies can focus on a survey and critique of negative imagery, such as Shakespeare's depiction of Richard III.[24] This approach, according to Mitchell and Snyder, made the case for the pervasiveness of disabled figures in literature, and thus provided significant justification for continued study. Since disability studies is so new to biblical studies, one can hardly avoid contributing to such an inventory. Nevertheless, a critique of negative imagery enters a funhouse when it comes to the Bible, a phenomenon to which I will turn in the conclusion. For the present, I note only that this necessary task is not the most important or interesting one. Mitchell and Snyder see the second approach as a corrective to the texts examined by the first: social realism tries to bring attention to inaccuracies in the representation of disabled persons, and instead tries to provide accurate representations. The latter would show, in a film for example, all the means by which deaf people navigate the social world, instead of making every deaf character a preternaturally

22. Schipper, *Mephibosheth*, 20.
23. Schipper (ibid., 21–22) also reviews this portion of Mitchell and Snyder's work. Since my purposes and emphases vary from his, I have proceeded independently with my own discussion.
24. See Shakespeare, *Henry VI, Part 3* V.vi.74–79, where Richard, then Duke of Gloucester, attributes his malicious nature to his malformed body.

talented lip-reader who never encounters communication barriers.[25] With respect to the Hebrew Bible, this tactic runs into the text's famously laconic quality. If the narrator does not tell us how Jacob manages his daily activities after acquiring a limp, does this absence of representation mean that the limp was temporary, or just that the author's attention to it was cursory? Many of these questions may not be resolvable. Third, new historicism within disability studies reconstructs the understanding of disability in different periods and socio-cultural contexts. Studies of the historical construction of normalcy fall under this rubric, where Mitchell and Snyder locate some of their own work, as well as Lennard Davis's. To the authors, this approach seems best suited to explore the paradox of disabled presence in representational arts and absence in the social world. The present work falls significantly under such a rubric, but not entirely so. I do not share the Marxist-influenced substrate of some forms of new historicism, but prefer instead an "old historicism" that recognizes and investigates the historicity of ideas. Further, with the Hebrew Bible, a certain tension between historical development and historical impact animates any investigation of a culturally important term (by which I mean the idea of God, not the idea of disability, although I shall argue a deep connection). A fourth approach, biographical criticism, is similar to the practice of "outing" within queer discourse. Many canonical authors were disabled, and yet canonicity erases disability.[26] Biographical studies seek to integrate disability into our understanding of the work of these authors, who include John Milton, Jonathan Swift, Alexander Pope, and Lord Byron, to list just a few writers from the Anglo-Irish tradition. Here, there is no problem of retrieving authors who were ignored, but rather of re-imagining some of the heaviest hitters in the canon as the blind, deaf, and lame people they actually were (to use the biblical trilogy of disability, and note its omission of cognitive and emotional impairments). Given the nature of the evidence for the Hebrew Bible, this kind of project is barely, if ever, practicable, although some scholars will not be deterred. The fifth and final perspective listed by Mitchell and Snyder should be familiar from other politically engaged fields of scholarship: transgressive reappropriation. As in other cases, this strategy ironically re-signifies derogatory terms and representations. It also critiques the omission of disabled bodies from even the most liberal discourse: the classical liberal emphasis on autonomy assumed a standard, able, adult body and said virtually nothing about the presence of disabled

25. Actress Marlee Matlin has been accused by some Deaf activists of acquiescing in just such a portrayal.
26. Mitchell and Snyder, *Narrative Prosthesis*, 30–35.

persons in the body politic;[27] and postmodernism has reveled in a representational body subject to infinite choice and pleasure, as if the choices of real bodies were not constrained.[28] For biblical studies, transgressive reappropriation may be the most loaded approach; in the conclusion, I shall discuss the difficulties this poses if one also wants to be historically responsible.

Concluding their survey, Mitchell and Snyder note that representation is inevitably political and informs the actual lives of disabled persons in a given time and place. They return to the paradox of prolific representation and social invisibility: "…whereas people with disabilities are often peripheral to domains outside of medicine, art persists in returning to portrayals of disability as a sustained preoccupation."[29] Why? Mitchell and Snyder set themselves just the task of answering that question in *Narrative Prosthesis*, which treats modern European and American literature and film. They find that disability functions as a narrative prosthesis: it provides the plot-inducing disruption, but remains unintegrated thenceforth. Some kind of repair of the disabled character then conceals the narrative's dependency on disability. I take as my task a similar question, in relation to the Hebrew Bible: what preoccupations with disability does it have, or do its constituent parts have, and how do these connect (or not) with its ostensible preoccupations—monotheism, divine power, purity, election, holiness?

### *Impairment and Disability in the Hebrew Bible and in Biblical Studies*

One might legitimately ask whether we can use these contemporary terms of the Hebrew Bible. Obviously, disabled persons appear in the canon. The common trilogy of "blind" (עִוֵּר), "deaf" (חֵרֵשׁ), and "lame" (פִּסֵּחַ) turn up in legal material, narrative, prophecy, and poetry. Other specific terms are abundant, as are descriptions of emotional and cognitive disabilities. Leviticus contains an interesting list of "blemishes," including skin diseases, uneven limbs, hunchbacks, and dwarves (Lev 21:17–20). Mental illness appears in 1 Samuel: David acts in a way that the Philistine king Achish thinks is crazy (מִשְׁתַּגֵּעַ, 1 Sam 21:13), while

---

27. Garland Thomson, *Extraordinary Bodies*, 42–43.
28. Although it contains many insightful essays, the collection edited by Timothy Beal and David Gunn sometimes succumbs to this pitfall. Timothy K. Beal and David M. Gunn, eds., *Reading Bodies, Writing Bodies: Identity and the Book* (London: Routledge, 1997).
29. Mitchell and Snyder, *Prosthesis*, 45.

Saul's detailed instabilities are never described with this term but rather as "an evil spirit from the Lord" (1 Sam 16:14). Nevertheless, since Biblical Hebrew has no single term that groups physical, emotional, and cognitive impairments the way "disabled" and similar terms do in modern cultures, the question arises whether the Israelites considered various disabilities to be disparate or related phenomena. Schipper considered the question most broadly in his examination of the concept in the ancient Near East.[30] He pointed to liver models and omen texts to demonstrate that Assyrian and Babylonian material both group various impairments or "abnormalities" together and also attribute meaning to them; thus we have neither numerous scattered specifics with no general concept, nor a neutral record of bodily variation.[31] With the Hebrew material, Schipper convincingly argues that the use of the internal noun pattern to form many terms for disabilities indicates an abstract concept. He lists other, non-disability uses of this pattern that seem to draw on the negative cultural valence of disability as further evidence of a general concept of "defects."[32] David Tabb Stewart also finds conceptual groupings in Leviticus and other Priestly material. He inventoried the Priestly terms and developed a taxonomy based on the four-fold schema generated by the intersections of "blemish" (מום) and "impurity" (טמא).[33] Like Schipper, Stewart concludes that the Hebrew texts do demonstrate an abstract concept of disability, albeit one governed by subcategories other than ours. I would further note the grouping of "blind and deaf" and "blind and lame," but never "deaf and lame" as evidence of higher-level concepts.[34] Blindness and deafness are both sensory impairments, and blindness and lameness both affect mobility; deafness and lameness do not share the same kind of obvious common feature. In short, the linguistic and textual evidence does support the existence of abstractions that grouped various impairments together, even though a single term

30. Schipper, *Mephibosheth*, 64–73.
31. Ibid., 70–73.
32. Ibid., 65–69.
33. David Tabb Stewart, "Deaf and Blind in Leviticus 19:14 and the Emergence of Disability Law" (paper presented at the Society of Biblical Literature, Philadelphia, November 19, 2005).
34. "Blind" and "deaf" appear in conjunction or parallelism in Exod 4:11; Lev 19:14; Isa 29:18; 35:5 (where the "lame" then follow in parallel with the mute), 18–20; 43:8. "Blind" and "lame" appear in conjunction or parallelism in Lev 21:18; Deut 15:21 (of sacrificial animals). 2 Sam 5:6, 8 (twice); Jer 31:3; Job 29:15; Mal 1:8 (of animals); Isa 59:10 and Zeph 1:17 mention blindness only, but describe it primarily as a mobility impairment. "Deaf and lame" never occur together as a pair, although they do rarely appear in the same passages, each with a different partner.

does not exist. One can compare the situation to that of "poetry" or even "religion" in the Hebrew Bible: Biblical Hebrew lacks terms equivalent to our abstractions, but it has abundant terms for the ingredients and the groupings that go into our abstractions.

Are the blind, the deaf, and the lame (and their other disabled companions) enough to justify a study of this sort? Most scholars who work in the field have been asked dismissive questions about the value of disability studies.[35] For this project, the question breaks down into two components: why study disability, and why study it in the Bible? Here are my short answers: because disability is a major human experience, and because the Bible contains the mother-lode of disability representation in Western culture. Both parts of this answer have long trains of thought, feeling, and life behind them. Before indicating more fully what those are, I turn to the development of disability studies within biblical studies.

Biblical studies has taken up the topic and task of disability only recently, but quite rapidly. Perhaps the first voice in this wilderness was that of Hector Avalos.[36] His 1995 monograph *Illness and Health Care in*

35. Lennard Davis's observations are perhaps the most pungent in print (*Normalcy*, xi–xii), and every scholar in my acquaintance can recount similar experiences.

36. The Jewish and Christian traditions have themselves grappled with disability, and would provide excellent areas for disability-related history of interpretation studies, along the lines of Nicole Kelley's work. Early scholarly interest took the form of medical history, for which Julian Preuss's *Biblisch-Talmudische Medizin* (Berlin: S. Karger, 1911; trans. by Fred Rosner as *Biblical and Talmudic Medicine* [New York: Sanhedrin, 1978]) remains a major source. Rosner later compiled the *Encyclopedia of Medicine in the Bible and Talmud* (New Jersey: Jason Aronson, 2000). Lynn Holden's catalogue of bodily deformities in the Hebrew Bible and early Jewish literature appeared in 1991 (Lynn Holden, *Forms of Deformity* [Sheffield: Sheffield Academic Press, 1991]). Norbert Lohfink showed some early awareness of the religio-medical context in a chapter of his *Theology of the Pentateuch: Themes of the Priestly Narrative and Deuteronomy* (trans. Linda M. Maloney; Minneapolis: Fortress, 1994), 35–95. The chapter is titled "'I am Yahweh, your Physician' (Exodus 15:26): God, Society and Human Health in a Postexilic Revision of the Pentateuch. (Exod. 15:2b, 26)." In 1998, Rabbi Judith Z. Abrams published *Judaism and Disability: Portrayals in Ancient Texts from the Tanach through the Bavli* (Washington, D.C.: Gallaudet University Press, 1998). Her approach considers representational elements, but not in a systematic way, and not yet in dialogue with the disability studies work that had come from literary scholarship. Tzvi C Marx's *Disability in Jewish Law* (New York: Routledge, 2002) examines the legal sources on disability, in an attempt to bring out the most humane elements of Jewish legal tradition in favor of the full human dignity of disabled persons. The historical-critical scholarship of the past decade will be discussed in detail below.

*the Ancient Near East* analyzed temples as parts of the health care systems.[37] Employing the model of medical anthropology, Avalos surveys a
wealth of texts and artifacts relevant to health care in the ancient Near
East. Avalos poses the following central question: "How does a socio-
religious conceptual framework affect and interact with the type of health
care that a society devises for its members?"[38] The framework includes
explanations of illness, possible remedies, and various consultants to
whom a patient would go for help. Collectively, the roles and practices
of any society constitute its health care system: "A health care system
may be defined as a set of interacting resources, institutions, and strategies that are intended to prevent or cure illness in a particular community."[39] This anthropological method avoids tendentious and unjustifiable
distinctions between "magic" and "scientific" medicine. At the same
time, Avalos employs Kleinman's distinction between disease and illness; the former term refers to biological processes, the latter to the
patient's experience. For example, temporal lobe epilepsy is a disease,
that is, a biological condition. In some societies, the epileptic might be
treated as a visionary, in others condemned as demonically possessed.
These social values would in turn influence the person's sense of having
an illness. What remedies, if any, one might seek would also be a part of
a larger symbolic and practical structure.

	Although Avalos's work focuses on health care generally, its rele-
vance to disability should be apparent. First of all, the method clearly
separates actual biology, to the extent that science is able to know it,
from social categories and values on the one hand and individual experience on the other. Societies and periods vary in the extent to which
impairment is medicalized, that is, relegated primarily to the health care
system. In turn, a health care system is embedded in a broader array of
religious, political, and social values. For example, if we take a standard
early twentieth-century, North American view of limb impairment, we
find that the person is expected to seek medical cures. Suppose a cure is
not available, and the impairment renders the person unable to work. In a
society that highly values personal autonomy and industrial economic
productivity, this person could be socially marginalized (absent independent wealth or a supportive family, the chances of becoming a beggar
are high) and also feel worthless. In a different kind of society, where

	37. Hector Avalos, *Illness and Health Care in the Ancient Near East: The Role
of the Temple in Greece, Mesopotamia, and Israel* (HSM 54; Atlanta: Scholars
Press, 1995).
	38. Ibid., 22.
	39. Ibid., 23.

personal value is not closely tied to labor or where types of labor that suit the person's body are available, the social placement and individual experience of the limb impairment would be quite different. How disability intersects or diverges from a culture's concept of illness also varies. Nevertheless, Avalos's study of ancient health care as a system provides a significant part of the large framework in which impairment and disability were understood in the Hebrew Bible.

Regarding ancient Israelite culture, Avalos concludes that the medical theology viewed God as the only agent and healer of illness. God's reasons for sending illness could vary, but the most frequent reason was to punish a transgressor. Thus, prayer and repentance were the major and possibly only acceptable strategies for seeking healing. Prophets functioned as the primary health care consultants, and their main activity was intercessory prayer. Temple officials did not play a major role in healing, and only confirmed health after healing occurred. In comparative perspective, Israel did not differ from its neighbors on the etiology of illnesses: divine provenance was the common view of the ancient Near East. However, Israelite monotheism and the centralization of worship in one temple had consequences elsewhere in the system. Specifically, many practices to which an ill Babylonian or Greek might resort fell under religious proscription in Israel. Further, where another inhabitant of the Near East might go to various temples of healing gods or goddesses, an Israelite had only one temple from which most illnesses would restrict access.[40] In general, these conclusions apply to physical impairment as much as to illness. In particular, the etiology of illness includes impairment too. Finally, Avalos's results provide a crucial historical context for literary study, for he has shown that the ancient Israelites, along with their neighbors, really did view God as etiology and cure: this cultural fact will be important in assessing the literal or metaphorical nature of various passages.

More recently, Avalos has proposed what he calls "sensory criticism," which he defines as "a systematic survey of biblical texts that would center on how different books, corpora, genres, and traditions value the natural senses…"[41] These valuations are implicated in a network of cultural symbolism. For instance, Avalos finds that Deuteronomistic literature highly values hearing and treats vision as suspect. His project is

---

40. Ibid., 407–20.
41. Hector Avalos, "Introducing Sensory Criticism in Biblical Studies: Audiocentricity and Visiocentricity," in *This Abled Body: Rethinking Disabilities in Biblical Studies* (ed. Hector Avalos, Sarah J. Melcher, and Jeremy Schipper; Semeia Studies 55; Atlanta: Society of Biblical Literature, 2007), 47–59.

not, strictly speaking, a disability studies analysis, but the shared area of concern should be apparent. In fact, the presence and function of a figure with a physical impairment often helps identify the sensory valuations of a given text or source. This proposed criticism blends well with the disability scholarship of Davis, Mitchell and Snyder, and Garland Thomson, and I shall employ it in tandem with their methods. Following Avalos, I bear in mind, for each genre studied, the question, "How does a given disability position a figure with respect to a text's highest concerns?" The answer will tell us something about how that stratum values or devalues different senses (Avalos's project), and thus how the body is used to construct, in religious terms, both a Normal body and a disabled Other (my project). Indeed, Avalos calls for a comprehensive investigation of the senses in biblical literature, a criticism on the order of source or rhetorical criticism. Although I endorse and hope to contribute to this enterprise, I see it not as a type of biblical criticism, but as a welcome step toward bringing biblical studies under the overall social-scientific method of religious studies.

Finally, the latest contribution as I write is Jeremy Schipper's *Disability Studies and the Hebrew Bible: Figuring Mephibosheth in the David Story*. Schipper deploys the full theoretical equipment of literary disability studies in a sustained analysis of the David narrative in the books of Samuel. Much previous biblical scholarship, Schipper argues, fails to perceive the text's or its own negative stereotyping of disabled figures. Thus he calls for further study in the negative-imagery mode listed by Mitchell and Snyder. More important, Schipper demonstrates the complexity of disability representation in the David narrative. He argues that Mephibosheth's disability, far from being a minor detail, provides an important site of ideological mediation on the nature of kingship and Davidic dynasty. Since I am attempting a more systemic approach to the Hebrew Bible, I will not examine any one genre or passage with Schipper's level of detail. However, I intend to expose a wider set of representations, valuations, and connections to key concerns, for the major genres of Hebrew biblical literature. Schipper's work is a methodological first: previous scholarship on the subject of disability was historical-critical or theological, but Schipper has produced the first book-length *disability studies* analysis of any portion of biblical literature.[42]

    42. The Semeia volume cited above represents, I believe, the arrival of disability studies on the biblical studies scene. It collects thirteen essays that treat various topics and could be divided into historical-critical and theological methods. For this reason, I shall not summarize or assess the volume as a whole, but rather shall refer to several of the essays in the chapters to come. As mentioned in the Acknowledgments,

## Method and Overview of the Project

As one would expect, the new scholarship on disability mostly follows the available trends already established in biblical studies: historical criticism, biblical theology, and postmodernism. These approaches tend to overlap in certain ways and not in others. For instance, a biblical theologian may accept or reject historical method. The one who accepts it may develop theologies of sources, or engage in a privileging of original forms, to the extent that those can be reconstructed (and even beyond that extent). One who rejects historical method engages in a protectionist strategy that places at least some faith claims above the knowledge-seeking enterprise. In turn, postmodern approaches tend to favor liberationist agendas rather than traditional forms of faith, but they proceed from epistemic assumptions that could just as easily support what might be called a "fundamentalist way of knowing." In emphasizing the role of the interpreter over that of the text, postmodernist approaches run the risk of constituting the text as mere prompt for contemporary fantasy. Among the reigning three, the historical method, by which I mean both textual analysis and archaeology, has made the significant advances in knowledge.[43] However, for reasons more sociological than intellectual, historical method within biblical studies has focused on the pre-canonical stage of regional history and literary development. Those who respond by defending the canonical form often have a theological purpose for doing so and may provide important critiques of historicist excesses; yet the canon is just as much an historical entity as its contributing steams were. I am well aware that this project could be construed to fall into a certain scholarly niche: the scholar-activist doing a postmodern, liberationist operation on biblical texts in a subject that has been largely ignored. But I do not find any of these standard approaches adequate for articulating my own intellectual commitments, nor do the assumptions, strategies, and purposes of liberationist readings suit this project.

Instead, I wish to ally myself generally with what Jacques Berlinerblau calls secular hermeneutics. In *The Secular Bible* (2005),[44] Berlinerblau articulates a secular biblical hermeneutics that proceeds from historical

Saul Olyan's *Disability in the Hebrew Bible: Interpreting Mental and Physical Differences* (Cambridge: Cambridge University Press, 2008) became available too late for me to use it in this monograph.

43. This case has been forcefully argued by John J. Collins in *The Bible After Babel: Historical Criticism in a Postmodern Age* (Grand Rapids: Eerdmans, 2005).

44. Jacques Berlinerblau, *The Secular Bible: Why Nonbelievers Must Take Religion Seriously* (Cambridge: Cambridge University Press, 2005).

methods and acknowledges established facts about the Hebrew Bible and respects these in its readings. He takes the well-established fact that the document is a trans-historical composite that could not have been intended by anyone,[45] and insists that biblical interpretation take this fact fully into account. As cardinal rules, biblical interpreters should avoid creating unity where there is none, discerning the intentions of a mind behind an historical strata (which is not an intentional agent), and taking the text's acknowledged polysemy as justification for making it mean anything we want it to mean.

Even among academic biblical scholars for whom the text's composite, redacted quality is beyond dispute, Berlinerblau finds what one might call a blessed rage for unity. Where are unity and intention to be found? If not in the whole, then in the parts, the semi-visible strata of deposits:

> For the majority of exegetes, the purpose of scholarly criticism is to recuperate the original sense of Hebrew Scriptures, its meant meaning, its intended message to humanity its essential truth. Even higher critics… aspire to declutter the witness, to tease out earlier textual strata, and to understand what the motivations were of the original authors and editors who they have uncovered.[46]

He calls instead for an abandonment of the quest for authorial intentions, not because these never exist, but because the motley nature of this text renders the task impossible. The Bible, according to Berlinerblau, amounts to a vector sum of a multitude of different intentions, and even if we could reliably decompose the vector elements that contributed to the sum, there is no intention to be found behind the resultant vector. Nobody meant *all* that.

I accept this much of Berlinerblau's analysis. Although an author with an intention is an historical fact, just as susceptible to historical method as anything else in history, we are not on the same evidentiary grounds when we ask what Winston Churchill intended in a given speech as opposed to what "the" Deuteronomist intended by "his" (or even "her") Moasaic speeches. Nevertheless, historical method has a role to play in secular hermeneutics. The conclusion that the document is composite, and far more so than traditional theological interpreters claim, is itself a product of historical analysis. Berlinerblau reminds readers that Wellhausen wrote of strata, not authors.[47] Thus, a modest use of the concept

---

45. Ibid., 30–53.
46. Ibid., 76.
47. Ibid., 33.

of strata and their historicity seems permissible, so long as we abandon the attempt to read authorial minds.

So we should expect polysemy, but should not run away with it. It may be the case that similar assumptions, thought structures, and values keep cropping up in different strata, or that a given stratum of material maintains a fair degree of consistency on some item. Even if the author and his or her intentions lie beyond recoverable evidence, the ideas themselves may be more susceptible to historical localization. In fact, a secular hermeneutics that does not need the text to come out some particular way may be best suited to locate these consistencies. Berlinerblau notes how the text always insists on a consistency it fails to display—and this feature runs through it. This peculiar lack of self-awareness, so to speak, *is* a consistency, which Berlinerblau calls its naïveté.[48] In this context, a historically grounded, un-theological, literary analysis of the Hebrew Bible should be possible.

As an historical project, then, this work examines the resultant vector of representations, precisely because this canonical representational system configures the categories—consistent or not—of later thought on disability. W. J. T. Mitchell defines representation as "…a triangular relationship: representation is always *of* something or someone, *by* something or someone, *to* someone."[49] He then places one triangle on top of another, so to speak, to form a four-term relationship that includes the represented, the means of representation, the maker of the means, and the recipient of the representation. Of literary representation, Mitchell says, "The 'means' of literary representation is language, but there are many ways of employing that means (dramatic recitation, narration, description) to achieve all sorts of effects (pity, admiration, laughter, scorn) and represent all sorts of things."[50] This apparently simple schema allows us to look for representational features of the biblical text, no matter the genre of a given book or passage. We are accustomed to distinguish historiography—works that at least intend to represent actual events—from the soaring rhetoric of prophecy at its least referential. Yet both genres have representational features, whether or not they claim to have or achieve factual accuracy. There was an Assyrian invasion; prophecy represents it as divine punishment for sins. Thus a "fact" occurs and is construed within a system of codes and valuations and loses its mundane

48. Ibid., 50, 66.
49. W. J. T. Mitchell, "Representation," in *Critical Terms for Literary Study* (ed. Frank Lentricchia and Thomas McLaughlin; 2d ed.; Chicago: University of Chicago Press, 1995), 11–22 (12; emphasis original).
50. Ibid., 13.

quality. In explaining his choice to focus on a character, Schipper notes that scholarship on disability has emphasized legislation, whereas narrative concretizes what the law must abstract.[51] Even law, however, has representational qualities. Consider the prohibition against insulting the deaf (Lev. 19:14). This command from an anonymous author speaking as Moses is addressed *to* hearing people; it *represents* deaf people as potential passive recipients of the actions of hearing people. Deaf people do not appear as speakers or addressées, and the law fails to imagine that the deaf person might become aware of the fact of insult, if not the precise contents, and respond with a few choice signs. No one commands that they may not, for they are not represented as agents.[52] If I seem to accuse an earlier age of excusable ignorance, consider the more recent history of the term "person," and the actual people who were not represented by it, in American law. Being legally represented *as* a person *to* other people means that one has arrived within the scope of "human" rights.

Mitchell describes two "challenges" (his word—I am tempted to say "evasions") of representation. The first attempts to subordinate or even denigrate the concrete means of representation in favor of something nebulous: "Expressionism generally posits an unrepresentable essence (God, the soul, the author's intention) that is somehow manifested in a work."[53] (The pitfalls multiply exponentially if someone advances a text as representing God's intentions for the soul.) This approach falls under Berlinerblau's critique of the habit of seeing more unity and intentionality than is there. Liberationist readings in defiance of philology and historical reconstruction also make use of expressionism. The second challenge, formalism, "emphasizes the representational means and manner—the materiality and organization of the 'signifier' or representational object—and de-emphasizes the other two angles of the representational triangle."[54] Early deconstruction would fall here; Mitchell classifies more recent developments that view everything as representations that never land on reality, so to speak, as fully postmodern. In biblical studies, such an isolating strategy, even when insightful, obscures the

---

51. Schipper, *Mephibosheth*, 8–9.
52. Oliver Sacks reports a visit to a deaf synagogue where the Yom Kippur prayers contained the following: "We have sinned through being impatient with the hearing when they failed to understand us." In this prayer, deaf Jews represent themselves as agents, responsible for the moral ramifications of communication. Oliver Sacks, *Seeing Voices: A Journey into the World of the Deaf* (New York: Vintage Books, 2000), 189–90.
53. Mitchell, "Representation," 16.
54. Ibid.

very real impact the Bible and its interpreters have on what we used to call reality. In any case, formalism does not adequately account for metaphor, which requires a sort of double-layering of the representational triangle. "Flesh is grass" does not seem to work unless I know what flesh and grass are, independently of this statement. While language does not refer to things in a simple way—it depends on a subjectivity, that essential third that actually constitutes the triangle (without subjectivity, there would be no line segment between the other two points), and it contains structural terms that express relations—the difficulties in fully describing how language operates do not warrant cutting it free from everything else. Although my study focuses closely on the text, it does so always with an awareness of what is being represented, and to whom.

In addition, representation helps us avoid certain unproductive lines of inquiry, in particular, a too-nice or too-garbled attempt to distinguish literal and metaphorical language. I do think that there is such a distinction, but it often operates in peculiar ways in biblical studies. Suppose, for instance, that some exegete comes to feel strongly that prostitution is a great good. We also stipulate that the exegete wants to maintain a version of biblical authority. This reader, for whatever reason, is reluctant to say, "The Bible is wrong, and I am right." So when she looks at Jer 2–3, where the term "whore" occurs in reference to Judah, she might (rightly) point out that the term is metaphorical. It is difficult to say how either a geographical region, or all the inhabitants thereof, might have sex with someone for compensation. Therefore, the implied negative valuations do not attach to prostitution per se, but rather to whatever the people of Judah were actually doing. So this kind of language does not count against prostitution, in our hypothetical exegete's hypothetical reconstruction of a biblical view. The trouble lies in the last inference: just because a term is used metaphorically, it does not follow that the negative valuation attaches only to the target of the metaphor. If anything, the opposite is usually the case: the extreme negative valuation of whoring is *exactly* what gets transferred from actual prostitution to the religious pluralism the text condemns. Conversely, literal language can be disarmed by interpreting it as metaphorical: the legislation about prostitution is passé, but we can render it still-meaningful by treating it as a metaphor for selling oneself to undeserving values. The biblical polemic against prostitution could become a critique of consumerism. In the context of a culturally authoritative text whose meanings are often distasteful to contemporary palates, the literal–metaphorical distinction can be worked both ways to save face. Perhaps representational analysis can keep us honest by providing enough distance to take the bite out of difficult or unpalatable, but nevertheless philologically assured, meanings.

Finally, the concept of representation renders aid when the literal–metaphorical distinction cannot clearly be made. Some cases are easy. When the legal language of Priestly literature refers to blemishes or visible wounds, there is no good reason to think that the compliers meant anything other than actual blemishes. On the other hand, the language of Isa 1:5–6 ("the whole head is sick and the whole heat faint. From the sole of the foot even to the head, there is no soundness in it, but bruises and sores and bleeding wounds…") does not signify any actual body, but uses a metaphor of the wounded body to signify the state of a corporate entity, Judah. It will sometimes be important, and sometimes difficult, to determine whether disability terms are literal or metaphorical. But what about the Psalms that begin with a petition that God not be deaf (e.g. Ps 28:1)? Or the sudden appearance of disabled persons in some passages of prophetic eschatology (e.g. Isa 35)? When terms for impairment appear, they can be either literal or metaphorical, but they are always representational. Literal terms represent impairment, even beyond the straightforward referent. Metaphorical terms represent something as something else, and in doing so, charge their subjects with certain valences. Further, the relevant terms are not limited to the obvious trinity of disabled figures, the blind, the deaf, and the lame. A much wider array of language for the senses and for the body must be included in order to articulate fully the biblical representations of impairment and disability.

In this context, one does well to register a warning. Meredith McGuire charged social-scientific religious studies with forgetting that human beings are bodies, and that we experience our bodies as ourselves. Against the conceptual-laden habits of scholarship, she noted what should go without saying: "…bodies *are* matter. The material reality of our bodies is part of the grounding of human experience in reality… Because bodies are matter in this second sense of the word, they are linked with other material realities."[55] If social scientists are apt to forget this, literary critics and religions studies scholars are at least as culpable. The Bible proposes various schematizations of the body, from its proper form and sensory endowment, to the proper habitual use of this form and those senses. The schemas depend entirely on the bodies we actually have; how could it be otherwise? There are no commandments warning us not to allow our sonar to lead us into sin, or not to use our electroshock stingers to harm others. Levites who are missing a wing are not proscribed from priestly performance. If these examples seem trivial, we

---

55. Meredith McGuire, "Religion and the Body: Rematerializing the Human Body in the Social Sciences of Religion," *JSSR* 29 (1990): 283–96 (284; emphasis original).

should carry them fully into how a scripture represents a god. As David Hume observed, all of our ideas, including those of God, ultimately come from experience:

> When we analyze our thoughts and ideas, however compounded or sublime, we always find, that they resolve themselves into such simple ideas as were copied from a precedent feeling or sentiment. Even those ideas which, at first, view, seem the most wide of this origin, are found, upon a nearer scrutiny, to be derived from it. The idea of God, as meaning an infinitely intelligent, wise and good Being arises from reflecting on operations of our own mind, and augmenting, without limit, those qualities of goodness and wisdom. We may prosecute this enquiry to what length we please; where we shall always find, that every idea which we examine is copied from a similar impression.[56]

And impressions, as Hume uses the term, come from the senses and the emotions—in other words, the body. One need not swallow Hume's philosophy whole to appreciate this point. To transpose it into disability terms, the concept of God's power walks on the human body as on a crutch; human beings make of themselves crutches in order to represent God as powerful. Hebrew thought could eschew polytheistic iconography, but it cannot fly free of this conceptual limitation. Nor can any later religious system. Even the abstract qualities of the God of the Hebrew Bible rest on descriptions of and analogies to an idealized human body.

This task will take us through several layers of the Hebrew Bible. Since I focus on bodily representations, I have chosen to limit this discussion to physical disabilities; cognitive and emotional disabilities are mentioned only occasionally. Chapter 2 treats the most categorical representations of disability, those found in the Priestly literature, especially Leviticus, and those of Deuteronomy and Deuteronomic thought. Both represent disability primarily in a legal context, yet important differences in Priestly and Deuteronomic representations appear. In Chapter 3, the focus shifts to disabled figures, the Patriarchs and Matriarchs of Genesis, and that paradigmatic sufferer, Job. There, I analyze the narrative and dramatic features of disability representation as it also represents God. Chapter 4 takes up the most dynamic use of disability imagery, that of the Psalms and the prophetic poetry of Isaiah. In these texts, disability is no longer a property of an individual, but a mode of representing communication itself. The conclusion, Chapter 5, will survey the terrain covered and assess the role of disability in relation to the Hebrew Bible's themes of election and divine power. There, I gather the evidence of the

---

56. David Hume, *An Enquiry concerning Human Understanding* (ed. Tom L. Beauchamp; Oxford: Oxford University Press, 1999), 97–98.

preceding chapters to argue the following thesis: disability plays an essential role in defining God's power and holiness, and Israel's election, to the extent that we can say that the Hebrew Bible represents a Normal God, that is, it represents God by means of the ideological body-Normal. The conclusion will also suggest some ways in which disability as a critical mode can contribute to biblical studies.

## Coda

Before setting out on this survey, I return to Lennard Davis. In his Preface to *Enforcing Normalcy*, after only five pages on defining disability, Davis anticipates that readers are already asking if he is disabled, and if so, how.[57] I too anticipate this response. The underlying assumption seems to be that only someone with a disability would be interested in the field. Disability studies has been largely, but not entirely, the work of scholars with disabilities. Whether that is good or bad, I cannot say. "Nothing about us without us" remains a credo of the disability rights movement, so the scholarship is one enactment of that idea. The best scholarship about disability that comes from people with disabilities has, in certain regards, far more experiential depth and analytical acuity than scholarship that cannot detect its able-bodied assumptions or imagine a disabled reader. This experiential weight can be compared to the differences between male and female knowledge about the experience of the male gaze, or African-American experiences of the significations of whiteness in the United States. But experience alone does not make good scholarship, and many major disability scholars are not themselves disabled. The difference lies in a certain point of view, not so much in imagining a disabled experience as in letting go of the Normal tyranny and paying more careful attention to the vagaries of human embodiment. We all begin life unable to walk, talk, or care for ourselves. Relative to the able-bodied adult, every infant and toddler is disabled. Then, if we live long enough, most of us will acquire at least some age-related deficits in vision, hearing, mobility, and cognitive function. When an individual regards his endowments as "normal," he excludes from his personal identity the different experiences at the beginning and end of life. (I use the masculine pronoun deliberately, as the best pronominal signal of the ideological Normal.) Suppose a man lives a lifespan of eighty-five years; some fifteen at the beginning and fifteen at the end entail some degree of what would be called disability if it occurred at a different time. Thirty years out of eighty-five is thirty-five percent of

57. Davis, *Normalcy*, xvi.

one's time on earth as something other than an able-bodied, "normal" (male) adult. An identity that ignores or denigrates that much of its time is a function of something other than statistics. More people should be interested, for disability is a major component of human experience, and not an isolated one.

But it is a major experience for some of us more so than for others. Even as I wrote the above paragraph, I know too well why I am sensitive to the timing of a disability. I have a progressive hearing loss that began in my early teens and had reached profound deafness by my mid-twenties, when I was in the thick of graduate school. Progressive deafness has influenced my life in many ways, and, although I was a hearing child, my experience of academe is primarily a deaf one. In my mid-thirties, I elected to have cochlear implant surgery. The combination of this machine and my brain's ability to use it has wrought a new stage of life that has no name. Most hearing people (which includes every scholar of religion I know, save one in training) experience me now as someone who can pretty much hear. This is true in most of the contexts of daily life. But hearing after deafness is not the same as hearing simple; it is not even "after" deafness.

As a deaf biblical scholar, I have had the experience of being signified (quite uncomfortably) by the text and also of being aware of the text's multifarious significations of deafness.[58] In graduate school, the copious use of deafness as a metaphor for rebelling against God washed over me without impact. Once I began teaching, some students reported that others regarded my deafness as the reason why I did not share their religious views.[59] Reading passages such as Isa 6 suddenly became fraught in a way it had not been years before. Yet what changed was not my hearing but my context: I had an audience that took the text to signify me, whether I thought so or not. This experience perhaps contributes to my extreme reluctance to dismiss metaphorical language as harmless, or to pretend that literal language is metaphorical. It also draws my attention to certain details or difficulties. For instance, the command in

58. Although I do not share his visual impairment, John M. Hull's *In the Beginning, There Was Darkness* (Harrisburg, Penn.: Trinity Press International, 2001) has the complexity of response to the biblical representations of blindness that I believe I experience toward its representations of deafness. For instance, when he discusses Gen 27, Hull knows first-hand the difficulty of deciding among competing senses and the risks of making a mistake.

59. I have addressed these topics at more length in "Academe Is Silent About Deaf Professors," in *The Chronicle of Higher Education: The Chronicle Review* (September 15, 2006), B12–13, and in "He Who Has Ears to Hear," *Spotlight on Teaching* 20, no. 3 (May 2005): x.

Lev 19:14 addresses hearing people, not deaf people, but it describes something I have experienced: coming to awareness of being insulted or screamed at in public. On the one hand, I appreciate its humane intent. Some people do approach others' disability as an opportunity to practice cruelty, and this should be deplored. On the other hand, the text imagines a deaf person who has no way of becoming aware of the insult and responding. I detect an audist[60] assumption in both the text and the commentaries, which view the deaf person as unable to return the insult, or assume that a visual-gestural language cannot carry the semantic value of a spoken curse.[61] Response is, of course, possible, but one must first imagine deaf agency. In short, I cannot pretend that I am hearing person reading the Bible; nor can I pretend to write for all Deaf and deaf persons.[62] But I do hope that my individual deaf way of reading will yield results of general interest.

60.   Audism is a common Deaf Studies term for attitudes and practices that privilege hearing and speech as the only possible or "right" means of communication. Later, I shall use the term audiocentricity for a high valuation of audition-orality that may or may not also negatively value the visual-gestural. Unlike audiocentricity, audism connotes purposeful exclusion.

61.   All of the following commentators mention or tacitly assume the deaf person's inability to respond: Erhard S. Gerstenberger, *Leviticus: A Commentary* (Louisville, Ky.: Westminster John Knox, 1996), 268; Jacob Milgrom, *Leviticus 17–22: A New Translation with Introduction and Commentary* (New York: Doubleday, 2000), 1639–40; Martin Noth, *Leviticus: A Commentary* (rev. ed.; Philadelphia: Westminster, 1977), 141; and Sarah J. Melcher, "Visualizing the Perfect Cult: The Priestly Rationale for Exclusion," in *Human Disability and the Service of God: Reassessing Religious Practice* (ed. Nancy L. Eiesland and Don E. Saliers; Nashville: Abingdon, 1998), 55–72 (Lev 19:15 is discussed on p. 69).

62.   In contemporary English, Deaf with a capital D indicates the Deafworld, that is, those who use a signed language as their mother hands, so to write, and who identify with the culture generated by this linguistic community. A lower-case "d" in deaf indicates someone who does not hear. I am, in the lingo, a late-deafened adult: someone who lost hearing after acquiring a spoken language as a mother tongue. Even this term has its limitations, for it suggests a hearing phase in adulthood, which I did not have.

Chapter 2

CATEGORIES:
DISABILITY CONTRA THE HOLY AND THE REAL

But he shall not come near the curtain or approach the altar, because he
has a blemish, that he may not profane my sanctuaries; for I am the Lord;
I sanctify them.

—Lev 21:23

The problem, unstated till now, is how
to live in a damaged body
in a world where pain is meant to be gagged
uncured      un-grieved-over.      The problem is
to connect, without hysteria, the pain
of any one's body with the pain of the body's world
For it is the body's world
they are trying to destroy forever
The best world is the body's world
filled with creatures      filled with dread
misshapen so      yet the best we have
our raft among the abstract worlds
and how I longed to live on this earth
walking her boundaries      never counting the cost

—Adrienne Rich, *Contradictions: Tracking Poems*, XVIII[1]

Priestly and Deuteronomic literature both think in highly categorical
terms about disability. That is, whatever tensions appear in these systems, they seem to assume, so deeply as to be unaware of the assumption, that everything about the body *can* be categorized in religiously
relevant terms. Further, both locate disability primarily in the individual
body. Priestly literature definitely does so, and Deuteronomy does so
while also apparently envisaging disability as a possible corporate

1. Adrienne Rich, "Contradictions: Tracking Poems, XVIII," in *Your Native
Land, Your Life* (New York: Norton, 1986), 100.

property. The common features of both systems are well known, and their respective accounts of disability generally fit with their overall habits of thought. Highly binary as both systems are, they nevertheless have their differences in how they approach the senses. To understand these differences, we must first note something about the relevant senses. For the sighted, vision provides the major sense of orientation in space.[2] Temporal awareness enters visual-spatial orientation through movement, which requires time. Yet the sacralization of space, locations, and bodies does not need, and usually does not include, time as an essential component of the sacrum. The Holy of Holies in the Temple, for instance, is sacred because of what it is and where it is; its use on holy days is a consequence, not a constituent, of its holiness. Audition, by contrast, requires time: it cannot exist without time, for the auditory phenomenon unfolds essentially in time. The Deuteronomic command to recite certain prayers (Deut 6:7) requires an oral-aural performance, and it takes time, which the command also specifies. So we should expect audiocentricity to go with a greater emphasis on time, too, that is, to find with it a tempocentricity. Finally, a source, document, or representational system that favors one of these over the other will thereby produce different possibilities both for a valenced taxonomy of disability and also for incipient narrative representation.

Following Avalos's proposed sensory criticism, we can describe the different sensory emphases of Priestly and Deuteronomic literature.[3] The Priestly literature emphasizes the visual-spatial sensorum. At any given time, a body can in principle be located in the system's binary categories of holy and profane, clean and unclean. Motion across boundaries introduces the modest presence of time in Priestly literature. Over time, movement across categories is possible; among impurities, some are temporary and remediable through ritual, while others are permanent. In Deuteronomic thought, the visual-spatial recedes in favor of a strong audiocentric and temporal emphasis. Communication between the divine and human occurs primarily in these media, rather than in a visual-spatial matrix. To view these emphases as mutually exclusive would be to

---

2. The vestibular system of the inner ear also plays a crucial role of which we are usually unaware until its function changes, temporarily or permanently. People who lose vestibular function speak of the difficulty of relying solely on vision for bodily orientation in space, but this skill can be learned. Our biblical sources show no awareness of this physiology and simply link spatial orientation with the sense through which we typically experience where things are in space.

3. Avalos has sketched out the general audiocentricity of Deuteronomy and the Deuteronomistic History in "Sensory Criticism," 50–55.

over-generalize, but a certain asymmetry should be noted: Deuteronomy overtly eschews the visual-spatial in away that Priestly literature never treats the auditory-temporal. Leviticus, for instance, lacks Deuteronomy's tendency to engage in polemics against the less-valued sense; it would be more accurate to say that Priestly thought ignores sound.

### *Disability Contra What?*
### *The Construction of a Priestly Norm*

In examining Priestly literature, we should bear in mind that it is doing many things. Superficially, it lays down regulations for cultic rituals and the officials responsible for their performance. In doing that, the literature also articulates a set of concepts about God, the holy, and the human. Further, these concepts are not neutral, but cast the entire world in highly value-laden terms. For instance, Olyan has analyzed how binaries, most clearly articulated in Priestly literature, also construct a social hierarchy in Israelite society.[4] The likely social ramifications are not the only further influences these texts and practices exerted. With respect to the body, Priestly literature has a lot to regulate, such that a human body may properly live within P-world. (By P-world, I mean the best-case cosmos as imagined by Priestly literature.) Since priests play such an important role, I shall focus primarily on them, and primarily in the book of Leviticus. The key question is this: in representing the priesthood and the sacrificial cult, what else does Leviticus represent about God, the body, and human disability?

Before proceeding to details, I should elaborate on the concept of regulation as representation. We moderns are accustomed to the idea that legislation should be achieved through representation (of a smaller group for a larger group); the idea of legislation *as* representation seems more remote. Yet it is unavoidable. The introduction suggested a representational analysis of Lev 19:14, and further examples from different times and places help clarify the idea. In the Code of Hammurabi, the prologue names the key deities, briefly refers to Marduk's naming of Babylon, and introduces the speaker, Hammurabi. It represents Babylon as a focal point of divine attention, and the king as the agent of divine justice. A long rehearsal of various divine and royal actions concludes thus:

---

4.   Saul M. Olyan, *Rites and Rank: Hierarchy in Biblical Representations of Cult* (Princeton: Princeton University Press, 2000).

> When Marduk commissioned me to guide the people aright,
>     to direct the land,
> I established law and justice in the language of the land,
> Thereby promoting the welfare of the people.
> At that time (I decreed)...[5]

Before the contents of statutory law appear, the representational setting has already been framed. But representation does not stop with the setting; the laws themselves also represent their societies, if not in exact detail, at least in aspiration.[6] The explicit social stratification of the Code represents not just a hierarchy of social status, but hierarchies of agency and responsibility. Consider the law for wives of deserters:

> If, when a seignior deserted his city and then ran away, his wife has entered the house of another after his (departure), if that seignior has returned and wishes to take back his wife, the wife of the fugitive shall not return to her husband because he scorned his city and ran away.[7]

Support for the deserter's wife is only one concern in this law, but if that were the only important idea, we would expect the law at least to permit, if not to require, return to the deserter, who can now support her. But support of wives is only one concern, and not necessarily the most important. Ostensibly about what the abandoned wife may do, this regulation also represents a right way of behavior for a lord, in which loyalty to one's city figures prominently. In short, the Code of Hammurabi includes both self-representational elements and representations of its values and ideals. For a modern comparison, one might consider how the United States Constitution represents itself as the will of "we, the people" (but who exactly was or is that?), assumes a highly acquisitive strain in human nature in its very attempts to check and balance power, and represents its citizenry as active individuals. Whether the citizens of the United States are thus accurately represented at any give time is another question. At the very least, every legal system contains an implicit anthropology, which the laws themselves cannot but represent. These representational features occur independently of historical compliance with the actual laws.

---

5.   *ANET*, 165 (section 5).
6.   In a brief aside on Hammurabi, David Tabb Stewart ("Deaf and Blind in Leviticus 19:14) remarks that the king seems more interested in showing his justice to the gods, rather than in making a real legal code. I agree with this observation, but do not think that it precludes the Code from having been intended as a legal system and even so, from representing other things.
7.   *ANET*, 171 (section 136).

For that reason, it does not matter a great deal to what extent the Levitical laws were observed. Even approximate execution of them would have enormous representational weight. Their historical setting matters insofar as it may have allowed extensive enactment, or expressed a memory, or aspired to a future instantiation. In what follows, I accept the scholarly consensus that the book of Leviticus and related Priestly literature reached their final redactions in the post-exilic period; they probably include more ancient practices, and surely express the ideals of their authors.[8] Holiness is arguably the central concept of Leviticus, and it is represented primarily by categorical separations. Leviticus 10:10 provides a key statement:

ולהבדיל בין הקדש ובין החל ובין הטמא ובין הטהור

You are to distinguish between the holy and the common, and between the clean and the unclean.[9]

As Milgrom notes, despite the chiastic sets of pairs, this verse does not propose a single opposition in two different ways; it proposes two distinct but related sets of opposing terms.[10] The categories holy/profane and pure/impure locate items in this structure; Lev 10:10–11 summarizes the priestly task as one of making and teaching these two distinctions. Milgrom schematized the possible interactions thus: the sacred–profane boundary is permeable, the pure–impure boundary is permeable; common things can be either pure or impure; sacred things can only be pure.[11] Further, Milgrom characterizes the operational thrust of the purity regulations thus: "…the goal is that the categories of common and impure shall largely disappear, by their respective conversion into the sacred and pure."[12] Leviticus literally has an agenda, that is, something to do. This agenda amounts to an attempt to conform human bodies, as much as possible, to the cosmic order. Anthropologist Mary Douglas has analyzed the analogical thinking of Leviticus, by which the sacred mountain, the Tabernacle, and the body mutually model each other and thus each

---

8. Israel Knohl, in *The Sanctuary of Silence: The Priestly Torah and the Holiness School* (Winona Lake, Ind.: Eisenbrauns, 2007), 1–7, argues for a post-exilic Holiness School redaction of Leviticus and of the whole Torah.

9. The similarity with Ezek 44:23 has been noted. Milgrom thinks that the author of Ezekiel knew this command, albeit not necessarily in the Levitical context (*Leviticus 1–16* [New York: Doubleday, 1991], 615). Noth also thinks that the similarity makes the texts post-exilic but not dependent in either direction (*Leviticus*, 69–70).

10. Ibid., 616.

11. Ibid., 616–17.

12. Ibid., 617.

instantiate the cosmic structure.[13] The contrast between bodily wholeness and bodily blemish intersects with these categories such that we can infer the value that Leviticus assigned to at least some kinds of disabilities. So, within this system of separations, I shall focus on two sites: the priestly body and the animal body. The material on bodily discharges will serve to gloss the concept of wholeness (תמים).

First, let us situate the priestly body within the matrix of disability analysis. In his discussion of the concept of a norm, Lennard Davis argued that ancient Greco-Roman art depicted ideal bodies, not normal ones. An ideal provided a composite image of the best features, but did not exist in actual bodies, nor was it the object of striving to bring the individual body into line.[14] Modern industrial societies, he argues, created the norm, that is, an ideological "average" body that most people, if not all, really were expected to have. Davis further notes that the ideal and the norm have different opposites, the grotesque and the disabled, respectively. For my purposes, Davis's contrast is useful, but requires some adjustment to account for ancient Israelite religion. Specifically, Leviticus constructs a priestly *norm* in that actual priests' bodies really are expected to conform to specifications. Historically, of course, this is not the modern industrial norm, but it has the relevant feature of real expectation on everyone encompassed by the rules. In contrast to the industrial norm, the priestly norm regulates a small subset of the population; since ordinary Israelites could not be priests, non-conformity to a norm could not disqualify them. On the one hand, it suits one's contemporary sensibilities that Priestly bodily strictures did not disqualify non-priests from non-priestly labor. But this assurance assumes that the priestly norm did nothing else beyond regulate the priesthood. As soon as we ask why these strictures, and just these, must be associated with the sacred, then we see many further implications. So, on the other hand, the priesthood seems to function more like a Greco-Roman *ideal* with respect to the general Israelite population;[15] through their construction of a human bodily ideal, the priestly norm represents God.

In order to perform the sacrifices and approach the altar, the priest must have not have any blemishes. The opposite of blemish is wholeness

13.   Mary Douglas, *Leviticus as Literature* (Oxford: Oxford University Press, 2000), Chapter 4, "Mountain, Tabernacle, and Body," makes the case for the triple mapping.

14.   Davis, *Normalcy*, Chapter 2, "Constructing Normalcy," especially 24–25.

15.   At least insofar as P strata tell us how priests wanted to be viewed; whether people actually regarded them in this way is another question. For a discussion of the gendered quality of disability in Leviticus, see Thomas Hentrich, "Masculinity and Disability in the Bible," in *TAB*, 73–89.

(חם): passages about which animals to sacrifice contrast these two terms (e.g. Lev 22:21). The passage concerning restrictions on blemished priests operatively and non-exhaustively defines blemish (Lev 21:18–20). The list includes blindness, lameness, facial disfigurement, uneven limbs, broken hands or feet, a hunched back, dwarfism, eye disease, skin disease, or crushed testicles. In an analysis of morphosemantic categories of blemished (מום), impure (טמא), and human (the unmarked case), David Tabb Stewart generates a four-fold scheme with a paradigmatic example for each category: impure blemish (skin disease); pure blemish (blindness); impure unblemished (separated); and pure unblemished (deafness).[16] The rules for priestly (and animal) disqualification focus on the first and second categories, whereas the fourth accounts for the omission of deafness as a disqualifier: it is located differently in the schema. In determining the Priestly Normal, the common features of the impure blemish category provide the key.

Commentators vary on whether they find any underlying concepts in this list. Milgrom, for instance, argues that the list is arbitrary and based on the animal list.[17] Even if this is correct, it simply pushes the question further back: does the animal list show any consistency? The animal list is less detailed; it does not mention hunchbacks or dwarves, among other things (Lev 22:19–25). Deafness, significantly, is missing from both lists.[18] Rather than hastily sweeping it under the rubric of something that is mentioned, we should ask how it differs in terms that Leviticus would find important. All the blemishes on both lists can be seen on an unclothed body, and no invisible deficits or variations are listed. While acknowledging that "A major criterion is appearance," Milgrom disagrees with Maimonides' opinion that all of the blemishes are visible.[19] His counter-example to visibility is the crushed testicle: he asserts that "the testes are not visible."[20] By this claim, I take him to mean that the priests did not perform rituals unclothed, such that this blemish is not

16. Stewart, "Deaf and Blind in Leviticus 19:14," 7–8.
17. Milgrom, *Leviticus 17–22* (New York: Doubleday, 2000), 1836–40.
18. Milgrom would not regard the omission as significant; he thinks that "obvious defects are not listed," and, to account for the term "blind," says that it must refer to the one-eyed (ibid., 1826). This strikes me as rather precious; it ignores the primary connotation of the term "blind," the frequent parallelism of "blind and lame," and, whether he wants to admit it or not, the common visibility of all items on both human and animal lists. It seems less a stretch to suppose that deafness was not categorized as a blemish, at least not at this time, than to suggest that "blind" means one-eyed here.
19. Ibid., 1825.
20. Ibid., 1825.

visible to others during the performance. But it is visible in the sense of what can be seen on the body.[21] In order for this rule to be enforced, someone would have to look.

Olyan cites passages about human beauty to note that blemished means ugly.[22] Nothing in Leviticus says that a priest (or an animal, for that matter) must be beautiful. Rather, ugliness renders the body unfit for sacrifice or sacrificial performance. Beauty is implied by the detailed description of its opposite. Thus, Leviticus associates holiness with physical beauty. The implied aesthetic criterion also helps explain the omission of invisible disabilities, for the deaf priest presents the same unruptured surface that a hearing one can. If ugliness makes a priest less holy (although still holy), then beauty makes him more holy. Yet beauty is only skin-deep, as they say, and some details require a deeper or at least more precise specification of the Normal.

Before elaborating on the visual qualities promoted by these restrictions, we should note from exactly what the blemished priest or animal is barred. Melcher draws a strong distinction between impurity and profaneness, arguing that the blemished priest is rendered profane, not impure.[23] Olyan makes a somewhat more nuanced distinction: he says that blemishes do not render a priest completely profane, just less holy, where there are degrees of holiness.[24] Since the blemished priest is allowed to eat the sacrificial food (21:22–23), he cannot be completely profane. Indeed, profanation does not attach to his body in itself; rather, profanation would occur if the blemished priestly body performed sacrifices or otherwise approached the altar (21:17, 21). The boundary-crossing or mixture seems to be the core of the problem. Again, the animal list provides some insight: offering a blemished animal is not in itself a profanation, but the offering is not accepted (22:21).[25] Some kinds of blemished animals are acceptable for some sacrifices (22:23). Were the

---

21.  Melcher ("Visualizing the Perfect Cult," 62–65) discusses the significance of visual criteria in the regulations about skin diseases that occur in Lev 14 but are not mentioned on this list. Specifically with respect to the Priestly list, Gerstenberger notes the visual common denominator (Gerstenberger, *Leviticus*, 316). Gerstenberger's commentary on these passages is unfortunately rife with unconscious and unquestioned ablest language and assumptions. Unlike Melcher and Gerstenberger, I do not find a strong pro-disabled view in Lev 19:14, for it speaks to and for an able-bodied audience and, although mitigating cruelty, does nothing to include disabled persons.

22.  Olyan, *Rites and Rank*, 103.

23.  Melcher, "Visualizing the Perfect Cult," 65–66.

24.  Olyan, *Rites and Rank*, 105.

25.  Noth, *Leviticus*, 162–63.

profane quality to inhere in the body itself, then the offering itself should
be a profanation, rather than merely inefficacious. In sum, human blemish at the altar is profaning; animal blemish on the altar is not accepted.
The human form is more highly valued, since its blemishes are more
harshly treated.

Although a visual criterion appears to be operating, it cannot be the
only factor. It does not explain why offering a blemished sacrifice is
something less than a profanation, while a blemished priest who performs
sacrifice is profane. Further, some items on the lists suggest criteria
beyond the simply visual. Dwarves are not disfigured in the sense of an
intruding injury to the body's surface.[26] Further, the animal list prohibits
animals with a discharge; this is not mentioned for the priests, who
would fall under the more rigorous regulations of human bodily discharges (which are impurifying but not profane). I suggest that these
details point to a deeper ideal than just visual aesthetics, an ideal that can
encompass not just the restrictions on blemished priests, but much else in
Leviticus.

Consider the restriction on an animal with a discharge (Lev 22:22) in
light of Leviticus' regulations about human bodily discharges. Discharges
are a significant site of movement from pure to impure. Gerstenberger
notes that the rules for discharges are specifically concerned with the
genitals, not other possible sources of discharge.[27] In most cases, purify-
ing rituals remove the impurity. Yet all discharges occur through bodily
orifices or interfaces more permeable, to ancient observation, than skin.
What about skin diseases (chs. 13–14)? Swelling or eruption, that is,
distortions in the body's surface, are key criteria in diagnosis (13:2).
Melcher notes a fascinating aspect of these regulations: if the skin turns
completely white with the disease, the person becomes clean (13:12–13).
She comments that "visual consistency and completeness is a more
influential factor" than skin disease.[28] What has changed is the sense of
rupture or mixture. Skin seems to be Leviticus' ideal boundary, as it
were, trying to convert everything on the body into skin. This idealiza-
tion of skin as boundary can encompass many of the discharge regulations and also many of the disqualifying blemishes of priests. Thus a
certain kind of surface represents holiness.

26. The translation is not certain. Milgrom (*Leviticus 17–22*, 1827), bases "a
dwarf" on the cognates. My observations would apply with little qualification to the
other proposals.
27. Gerstenberger, *Leviticus*, 194–95.
28. Melcher, "Visualizing the Perfect Cult," 64.

Finally, the presence of animals allows us to infer a species criterion at work. The graver consequences for priestly blemish, compared to animal blemish, indicate a privileging of the human form. And the exclusion of dwarfs, hunchbacks, and those with uneven limbs reflects an underlying concept of "correct" stature and symmetry. Size and symmetry, although visible, are not simply visual phenomenon. They reflect a sense of right proportionality, one based on the non-disabled human male. If blemish is the opposite of wholeness, and the most obvious blemishes are the ones listed, then wholeness means a body with a smooth, symmetrical, unruptured surface, on a frame of the right species, gender, and size.

The concept of gradient values for bodies or body parts appears in Douglas's work on Leviticus. Bodies, human and animal, have more and less important parts, according to how a given part models something somewhere else in the structure.[29] For instance, the innards of the sacrificial animal and the Holy of Holies both lie "at the point of highest esteem."[30] She glosses this correspondence with the high value the Bible places on inner parts as the seat of the being, subject to God's penetrating gaze. Perhaps the concept of blemish distinguishes bodies for which this order of outer/inner, or ostensible/hidden does not seem to hold. In this context, the emphasis on smoothness and symmetry fits well with the Body/Tabernacle correspondence: instructions for the Tabernacle require an exacting artistic skill, smooth substances, and symmetrical and hierarchical architecture. It is less clear how the required lack of visible disabilities would fit into the Body/Mountain correspondence, unless the common element is strength.

Finally, there is the question of audience. Who does Leviticus address? Noth notes that the rules about blemished animals are addressed to laypeople, who need to know what to bring.[31] However these rules were communicated, orally or in writing, we can suppose some dissemination, and thus some knowledge of the Levitical concepts of wholeness and blemish. And, whoever beyond the priesthood actually gained knowledge of the cultic regulations, Leviticus constructs its implied audience as the lay Israelite who needs to know the purity regulations for everyone and who needs to participate appropriately through animal offerings in the cult. Most of all, the constant reiteration of divine identity and the imperative to be holy assumes an audience that understands these

29. For instance, Douglas is able to offer a persuasive explanation of why the suet, of all things, is forbidden (Douglas, *Leviticus as Literature*, 71–76).

30. Ibid., 80.

31. Noth, *Leviticus*, 162–63.

demands and wants to fulfill them.[32] Meeting the requirements entails a rigorous but entirely possible bodily regimen.

What, then, is the Priestly Normal? It is a male body of a specific ancestry, having no visible blemishes. Even among priests, holiness comes in different degrees, and the more disability, the less holiness. Why should blemish be inversely proportional to holiness? In a cult that eschewed visual iconography, the visible representatives of God would be the sacred precincts and the priests. These elements of beauty, symmetry, and unruptured boundaries (skin) are represented as holy, or holier, where holiness is the definitive divine property. God is inherently holy, all the time; other beings only approximate the divine holiness.[33] But how would anyone know the contents of holiness, apart from the cultic representation of it? The specific features of the priestly body fill up what might otherwise be a vague or even null concept. Whatever else holy means, it means order, symmetry, and clear boundaries, perhaps even beauty. Symbolism provides no cover here, for we must explain why, exactly, an unblemished body symbolizes holiness more, or more accurately or fully, than an unblemished one, as Leviticus clearly indicates. If symbols are arbitrary, there can be no reason for regarding some kinds of bodies as holier than others; all would signify. Leviticus is not arbitrary in this way. If we recall McGuire's injunction, mentioned in Chapter 1, to remember that the body is material,[34] we have to face the fact that Israel did use material means to represent its God. How can anyone do otherwise? In this respect, the difference between impurity and profaneness diminishes, for both diverge in different ways from the ideal, and both by implication converge on the ideal as what they are not. The result is not two distinct concepts, the pure and the holy, but rather two facets of the same concept of Normal. The materiality of that representation values unblemished bodies and devalues, to different degrees, blemished ones. This is not about taking language literally, but rather about taking human thought concretely when it is concrete. Or I could suggest another way of looking at stock ideas backwards: if priests must be god-like, then God must be priest-like.

---

32. I disagree with Melcher's claim that holiness is unattainable by laypeople ("Visualizing the Perfect Cult," 57). If it is not, the explicit demands that the people be holy, together with detailed instructions about how to do just that, make no sense. Leviticus holds out holiness not just as a human possibility, but as an Israelite imperative.

33. Robert Hodgson, Jr., "Holiness," *ABD* 3:237–48.

34. Page 24, above.

## True Gods and Disabled Idols:
## Deuteronomic Bodily Polemics

If Leviticus represents God through the surface of the human (priestly) body, then Deuteronomy does so through the senses and their powers. As with Leviticus, the divine category is defined mainly in contrast to its opposite, namely idols. Here, I would like to examine the role of disability in articulating one of the Hebrew Bible's central categories, the distinction between Israel's one God and the gods of others. In particular, Deuteronomy and Deuteronomic literature deploy representations of disability to construct non-Israelite gods—"idols"—as disabled, in contrast to which Israel's God is able-bodied.

In his commentary on Deuteronomy, Moshe Weinfeld contrasts Deuteronomic and Priestly thought about the divine thus: "The elimination of the provincial cult permitted the transformation of Israel's religion into a more abstract religion, one that minimized external expression."[35] Deuteronomy, he notes, conceives of the Temple as the place where God's name (but not God) dwells; Deuteronomic theophanies downplay visual description and emphasize auditory phenomena.[36] While these comparisons certainly reveal a major difference between Priestly and Deuteronomic thought, Weinfeld's analysis is marred by a tendency to praise Deuteronomy for its alleged abstractions: he calls its conception of ritual "more rational" than that of the Priestly codes,[37] and remarks "the severance of these laws from the realm of myth and magic"[38] exemplified by the Passover legislation. The absence of physicality and myth (an association that itself deserves question), however, may be more apparent than real. One should avoid excessive haste in reading concrete terms as metaphorical abstractions. In fact, a disability analysis of Deuteronomy's conception of divinities can demonstrate the book's dependence on physical, concrete terms for its articulation of Israel's God.

### The Disabled Construction of Idols
The physicality manifests when we apply the concept of the Normal to the construction of the true god–false god dichotomy. Recall that the Normal cannot be constructed in a vacuum, but depends upon the

---

35.  Moshe Weinfeld, *Deuteronomy 1–11: A New Translation with Commentary* (New York: Doubleday, 1991), 37, with the full context continuing to p. 44.
36.  Ibid., 37–38.
37.  Ibid., 42. Douglas criticizes the tendency to view priestly thinking as irrational when it is merely analogical (*Leviticus as Literature*, 15–20).
38.  Weinfeld, *Deuteronomy*, 44.

existence and construction of its opposite figure. In fact, Garland Thomson notes that the normate (her term), as the unmarked term, tends to invisibility and assumed transparency; its specifications can only be determined by the prolific representations of what it is not.[39] To apply this concept to Deuteronomic literature, I will examine the marked term first, and then ask what these markings disclose about the Normal.

First, let us examine the terms Deuteronomy uses for other gods. The rhetoric repeatedly warns its audience not to follow other gods (Deut 13:2; 17:3; 28:14, 34, 36; 29:26). Beyond "otherness," Deuteronomy systematically adds terms indicating human artifice. The most common of these is "wood and stone" (28:36, 64; 29:17, or some variation on the phrase "made by human hands" (4:28, etc.). Forms of פסל, "idol," cluster in ch. 4 (vv. 16, 23, 25) and are scattered elsewhere (5:8; 27:15), along with less frequent terms such as סמל, "likeness" (4:16) and תמונת, "figure," (4:16, 20). Finally, the curses in Deut 28–29 also include in the concept of idolatry the notion of a god or a nation whom the Israelites "did not know" (28:36, 64; 29:26). Thus, Deuteronomy's language for the concept of idolatry not only emphasizes but links terms for foreignness, materiality, and artifactuality. Of the passages that combine several phrases and terms for the concept of idolatry, most of them appear in an editorial layer that Mayes identifies with an exilic redaction of Deuteronomy.[40] Weinfeld, while stressing the antiquity of the concepts elaborated here, notes that "sarcasm about manmade idols is found in the Pentateuch only in Deuteronomy...but is very common in the prophetic literature...and especially in Deutero-Isaiah..."[41] Historically, then, Deuteronomic thought about idolatry seems to have been elaborated in this manner just before and during the exile; after that, it influences exilic and immediately post-exilic prophecy.

Yet commentators fail to push further in examining the thought structure behind all this dwelling on wood and stone. Later ages of more abstract monotheism would employ existential claims and their negations, asserting that God is real and Athena (say) is not. But Deuteronomy is far from this level of abstraction. If the book can be called abstract relative to Priestly literature, it nevertheless employs concrete terms to articulate its central distinction between Israel's God and idols. Avalos argues how, in eschewing the visual, it relies greatly on the

39. Garland Thomson, *Extraordinary Bodies*, 40, referring to Foucault.
40. A. D. H. Mayes, "Deuteronomy 4 and the Literary Criticism of Deuteronomy," *in A Song of Power and the Power of Song* (ed. Duane L. Christensen; Winona Lake, Ind.: Eisenbrauns, 1993), 195–224; reprint from *JBL* 100 (1981): 23–51.
41. Weinfeld, *Deuteronomy*, 205; citations omitted.

auditory as the mode of revelation (4:12).[42] In its religious polemics, Deuteronomy repeatedly mocks the visual and tangible (see the verses cited in the preceding paragraph). To construe the text's auditory/visual distinction as an abstract/concrete distinction is to accept at least one of the premises of its polemic, that audition is less physical, less material, than vision. But this is not the case, nor it is exactly the text's major distinction. Deuteronomy says that the idols—concrete, material, visible things—are not real, or at least not really what people think they are.

What is the point in mocking physical representations? Israel also had cult objects made of wood, stone, silver, and gold, and Deuteronomy retains the verb פסל for how Moses gives the aurally received law a concrete form (Deut 10:1, 3, the command to engrave the law, and his performance of it). The Deuteronomic distinction, then, is not about the mere use of material or the role of human labor in creating an artifact. The passage in Deut 4 states the implications: it exhorts the audience not to forget God and not to make idols, on pain of dispersion from the land where they will end up worshipping idols in any case (4:23–28). One would think wood and stone's lack of senses goes without saying, yet Deuteronomy reiterates it often. For Deuteronomy, the material bodies of idols incarnate, as it were, certain qualities of those gods, specifically, the *inability* to see, hear, eat, or smell. Conversely, foreign gods are limited by their bodies such that wood and stone are all there is to them. Thus physics becomes metaphysics. A sort of negative anthropomorphism operates in these categories: idols are defective because they do not have the human senses attributed to God, and defect denotes lack of reality. Deuteronomy's God, by contrast, does hear, see, and act. (I might add, though, that he seems uninterested in smelling, at least compared to the God of priestly sacrifice.) Far from being a minor affair, disability figures prominently, perhaps centrally—and negatively—in Deuteronomy's distinction between God and idols. In short, idols are disabled, and, by implication, Israel's God is not. This Deuteronomic language leaves its imprint in Jeremiah and in other passages. Most notably Ps 115:4–8 draws together much that Deuteronomy disperses and repeats in snippets: idols are artifacts that cannot speak, see, hear, smell, feel, walk, or make a sound.

A disability analysis can expose the significance of these images and their connection to the overall thought structure of Deuteronomy. If we look for the Normal, we find that Deuteronomy constructs an able-bodied God primarily by constructing idols as disabled human beings. In fact, constructing the Normal by implication, rather than by direct statement,

---

42. Avalos, "Sensory Criticism," 51.

suits Deuteronomic religious thought perfectly. Recall Weinfeld's claim that Deuteronomy's representation of God is more "abstract," in support of which he cites the book's overwhelming preference for auditory rather than visual theophany. Deuteronomy is clearly allergic to visual representation of its deity, and it equates visuality with materiality in a way that Weinfeld fails to question. Deuteronomy's insistence that Moses and the people heard God's voice suppresses the question of how that vocalization was produced. Nor does it require a modern understanding of acoustics to know that sound is a physical phenomenon, produced by bodies and objects; the Deuteronomic characterization of sound as non-material, in contrast to the materiality of idols, is ancient ideology, not ancient science. Thus, for Deuteronomy, alterity *is* matter that can be seen and manipulated by artifice, and that cannot itself receive sensory impressions or act; by implication, the Normal is non-visual and superlatively sensate, seeing and hearing everything, and not subject to human artifice.

Further, the association between representation of Israel's God and the prohibitions against idolatry are not accidental. As Weinfeld notes, Deuteronomy spells out a link between these that is not present in the Tetrateuch. Commenting on 4:15–22, he notes: "This passage constitutes a warning against idolatry and looks like an elaboration of the second commandment of the Decalogue. The prohibition of idolatry is motivated by the fact that the revelation at Sinai was achieved without the appearance of the divine person of the use of any image..."[43] In other words, Deuteronomy represents the true God (polemically) only in auditory theophanies; it then uses that representation to justify its prohibitions on visual representations of gods; it mocks idols for being only the stuff of which they are made, and therefore, not able to do what a real God can do, that is, as disabled; and finally, it implies God's abilities precisely on the basis of God not having a material body. Thus, the contrast of Israel's God with others' idols is articulated mainly by the construction of a Normal (non-visualizable) body for God and a disabled body for idols: the God of Israel sees and hears superlatively well, and acts with superlative efficacy, whereas idols are completely deficient in the same ways.

*Deafening Deuteronomy*
But what is Deuteronomy made of? About all writing, Lennard Davis observed:

---

43. Weinfeld, *Deuteronomy*, 205.

The text itself is neither silent nor auditory. It is the phantasm of sound,
an insubstantial echo. It is a go-between linking the silence that surrounds
it to the auditory world. Writers write in silence; readers read in silence.
What they write and read they hallucinate into sound. But the sound is a
silent sound. The Zen riddle about textuality would be: What is the sound
of one person reading?[44]

Careful attention to Deuteronomy's audiocentricity uncovers some deep
disjunctions in the Hebrew Bible. In the context of its religious polemic,
not only does Deuteronomy represent hearing as the best receptive mode
for divine sound, but it suspects other senses as the source of deception,
even infidelity. Yet the Deuteronomic audiocentricity rests on a major
fault line between hearing and sight: Deuteronomy is a piece of writing,
a visual artifact, that wants to convince us that it is really sound.

Although the passages discussed here play an important role in studies
of the shift from orality to literacy, my interest lies in the underlying
valuations of the different sensory modes. The question is not merely
whether hearing is valued over seeing in general, but rather whether one
is considered extremely reliable, and the other not, for communication
with God. Now, whatever its oral–auditory antecedents, Deuteronomy is
writing. Other than the Song of Moses, it does not contain much material
that is likely to have been orally transmitted. Most scholarly debate
concerns its redaction history, that is, its genesis and evolution as the text
we now have. Yet the pretense of speech constitutes its main claim to
Mosaic authority: virtually all the book is direct discourse, from Moses
to the assembled people. In the narrative, the text represents oral performance first, and writing of the Teaching only afterward (Deut 31:9).
Further, the setting joins initiating speech to an initiating moment, at the
conclusion of the wandering in the desert and before the entry into the
land (into which the initiating speaker will not go). The fiction of original
speech thus attempts to provide an auditory foundation from which to
launch Deuteronomy's kind of religiosity and its concomitant critique of
visuality.

Two other initiating moments should be considered. The first, in
2 Kings, narrates the discovery of a "scroll of the Torah" (22:8) during a
temple inventory ordered by King Josiah for other reasons. That is, an
object comes to the attention of sight first. This scroll will find two readers, one pivotal non-reader, and a multitude of hearers. First, the priest
Hilkiah gives it to Shaphan, who reads it, apparently out loud (קרא), and
then reads it again before the king. The latter—the crucial—reading must
be an oral performance: Shaphan reads it to the king (22:10). Shaphan,

44. Davis, *Normalcy*, 117.

then, is the first reader and the one for whom the scroll as visual object precedes or coincides with his auditory perception of it. Josiah's reaction to the oral performance emphasizes his auditory perception (22:10b–11). Hilkiah and Josiah are both protected, so to speak, from a visual encounter with the scroll's writing, but somebody has to have that perception. Shaphan mediates between visual and auditory modes, for both high priest and king.

This hearing, however, is not enough. Josiah sends emissaries to the prophetess Huldah to ask about the scroll. Huldah never sees or hears this scroll; as visual object and oral performance, the scroll is absent. The messengers speak to her about it, and she responds with an oracle endorsing the scroll. In effect, the Deuteronomistic History (DtH) represents living speech, unmediated by a visual object, as the necessary warrant for the scroll's authority. After first describing an inevitable disaster, Huldah tells the king that, because of his response to what he *heard*, he will be spared from *seeing* a great disaster (2 Kgs 22:18b–20a). In terms of sense criticism, the oracle praises Josiah for his hearing and for its proper use. The divine response, then, is twofold: God in turn hears Josiah, and spares him from a certain sight. The obvious meaning is that the disaster comes after Josiah's time. However, the temporal displacement of disaster achieves an implicit sensory valuation, for Josiah's entire comprehension of this scroll, including the future enactment of its curses, is auditory. After all, one also hears of disasters, but the text selects sight as the medium through which this experience will not come. It comes, before the fact, by hearing. Thus, Josiah's understanding gets into him untouched by his own visual experience.

In effect, Huldah the prophetess stands in for Moses: through her, DtH represents the Mosaic mode of reception, a direct line to divine communication either before the text (visual or auditory) or in its absence. Up until this point, Josiah has also avoided a visual encounter. Only after both his fully auditory reception of the scroll and its text-free endorsement does Josiah become a reader, now holding Shaphan's role, to the assembled people (2 Kgs 23:2–3; cf. Deut 6:5–6; 30:16). Note both the distinction and the linkage between audition and vision. The people receive the scroll solely in auditory form, and yet they promise to follow its written contents, that is, the visual object. The appeal to the heart and mind, then, comes through hearing, but the enactment of obedience requires the detail of written text, and with it, visuality.

At every point—in Deuteronomy itself and in the key passages in Kings—the Torah is represented as speech first of all, and secondarily as writing, and hearing is represented as the best mode of reception. The written scroll seems both embarrassing and indispensable: embarrassing because of the efforts to consign it to the status of a prop, indispensable because it really is the means of transmission, stability, and enactment. To these observations, I now want to apply a combination of Berliner-blau's secular hermeneutics and Davis's deafness as a critical mode. Berlinerblau points out what he calls the text's naïveté: "our polysemous text does not only want to be read, listened to, and understood, but it also wants to be read, listened to and understood *the right way.*"[45] Here, Berlinerblau means consistent meaning; the Hebrew Bible claims to have a coherence in the contents of its teachings, an appearance belied by the blatant incoherence of the text.

Deuteronomy may be a moment of awareness of incoherence betrayed by the attempt to cover it up. Further, the specific cast of Deuteronomic incoherence cannot be fully captured by Berlinerblau's general analysis of the Hebrew Bible. Here, the sensory hierarchy and its religious valences emerge from the Deuteronomic ideology and are not necessarily applicable to other biblical strata. The audiocentricity itself is uncomplicated; if someone thinks that hearing is the only reliable sense through which to receive divine communication, so be it. The difficulty appears when one makes, even over-insists, on this claim for something that must first be visually perceived—a scroll, a writing, a text—and remain so. Deuteronomy and DtH want to be *heard*, and heard in the right way. In this case, the right way includes pretending, along with the text, that the visualizable text is somehow dispensable or secondary. Deuteronomy asks its readers to hallucinate sound, and then to be unaware of doing so through a visual prompt.

This observation returns us to Davis' concept of deafness as a critical mode. It goes without saying (in more ways than one) that Deuteronomy assumes a hearing Normal, and does not acknowledge that it may have deaf recipients. One could read the prolific occurrences of שמע and its forms as metaphors, but the text does not often use them that way. On the contrary, Deuteronomy isolates and elevates hearing as a central component of its polemic against idolatry: what cannot speak cannot be heard, and therefore, cannot be real. Deuteronomy drives a sensory wedge between idols and Israel's God, in that idols can be seen, touched, and even smelled and tasted if one is so inclined, but cannot be heard, whereas God cannot be seen, touched, smelled, or tasted, but can be—can only legitimately be—heard. Given Deuteronomy's representation of hearing as the only legitimate means of receiving divine communication, how could a deaf person receive its message? In the book's long listing of diseases and impairments as punishments, deafness never appears. In

45. Berlinerblau, *Secular Bible*, 66 (emphasis original).

contrast, it crops up in every other Pentateuchal book and stratum.[46] In short, we have in Deuteronomy a valuation of the body so audiocentric that deafness cannot even be named, precisely where one might expect it to be the worst calamity.

I do not mean to point out such an obvious exclusion of persons, much less bother to deplore it. The deeper significance of Deuteronomic audiocentricity becomes clear if we consider just how far deafness would undermine this claim to authority. The actual deaf person is only the beginning of the difficulty. Such a person must take in Deuteronomy visually, either in signed language or in writing, but in either case, visually. She or he would then take in a book that represents the very means of its reception by a deaf reader as illegitimate. There is no way for a deaf reader to hear Deuteronomy according to its own account of the right way to hear it. But how many people are deaf readers? In his discussion of the deafened moment, Davis means something other than inability to hear or the use of signed language:

> the deafened moment is one that does not rely on either the Deaf or the deaf... By the deafened moment, I am speaking (writing) of a contextual position, a dialectical moment in the reading/critical process, that is defined by the acknowledgement on the part of the reader/writer/critic that he or she is part of a process that does not involve speaking or hearing... [E]ach of these three entities [critic, reader, text] has a deafened moment that has been historically suppressed.[47]

For Davis, all readers, when reading, enact a deafened moment. It is precisely the acknowledgment of this fact that Deuteronomy strains to suppress. But why? I, a deaf reader, glance over at my BHS, and I see an object that neither sees, nor hears, nor smells, nor walks, nor speaks. Writing, in its visuality, is all-too-close to idols. In all likelihood, no one heard this text in its entirety before *it* was written down—its triply-iterated auditory origin myth notwithstanding.

### The Body Blessed and Cursed
Garland Thomson, and other disability theorists, usually analyze the representation of human bodies, that is, ideological attributions to actual bodies. Thus it may seem counter-intuitive to employ a term like Normal for a God who is not supposed to have a body in any ordinary meaning of that term. Although I believe that Deuteronomy's representation of

46. Forms of חרשׁ occur in Gen 24:21; 34:5; Exod 4:11; 14:14; Lev 19:14; Num 30:5, 8, 12, and 15 (three times), where it tends to indicate muteness or intentionally setting aside a prior speech act (vow).
47. Davis, *Normalcy*, 101–2.

God depends, not just incidentally but crucially, on its representation of idols as disabled bodies, further justification can be found in its representation of human health and illness. Specifically, the covenant curses in Deut 28 demonstrate a close association between idolatry and bodily disease and disability. Scholars have long noted that the afflictions listed in the curses are a stock ancient Near Eastern List of Bad Things, taken over from Assyrian documents. But source is not significance: the question is, what role do these afflictions play in the Deuteronomic economy of divine–human relations?

First, let us examine the content of the curses. As many scholars have noted, the covenant curses in Deut 28:16–19 directly negate the blessings of 28:3–6; these may form an early core of covenant blessings and curses. Along with invasion, subjugation, and loss of agricultural productivity, the section from v. 20 to v. 37 returns repeatedly to disease and disability, as if it were the center of the vortex of disaster. The passage then describes meteorological and geological decay, and an invasion. After a gory image of carrion birds feeding on the corpses of the cursed, the text alludes to the plagues of Egypt (28:27–28). These conditions set the stage for the next passage, in which others always interpose between an Israelite and some good. The pericope in vv. 47–57 describes siege conditions. At v. 58, there is a transitional phrase that marks the passage as the summary; it does not waste time with bad crops and invasions, but cuts straight to physical debilitation (28:58–60). There follows an unenumerated afflictions clause (28:61). Alongside disasters on the order of invasion and exile, this repetitious return to lingering descriptions of disease and disability is extraordinary. What is an itch, compared to the destruction of a city and the displacement of its population?

The answer, I suggest, lies in what activities these curses are supposed to punish. For Deuteronomy, failure to obey the commandments does not mean that the disobedient party is doing nothing; operatively, disobedience is defined as idolatry. In the covenant curses, idols make their curtain call as the definitive act of disloyalty. The blessings conclude with the operative definition that not turning away from the commands and not following other gods are different ways of saying the same thing (Deut 28:14). After the second major passage of physical afflictions, the list concludes with the warning that disobedience will result in conquest and being forced to follow artifactual gods (28:36). Again, in the summary, the unenumerated afflictions clause is followed by a contrast of the former, blessed and healthy state, with exile, the worst part of which appears to be idolatry (28:64). If scholarship is correct—and I believe it is—in dating this particular layer of Deuteronomy to the exile, then the association of dispersion with the danger of idolatry forms a coherent set of concerns that fit perfectly with exilic conditions. Further, the mockery of idols, which goes beyond the older prohibition of images, also makes sense in an exilic context. Scholarship has long noted the logic of a conditional land-grant with exile as the penalty for violating the conditions; valid as that insight is, it does not explain the extreme prominence of disease and disability in Deuteronomy. Nor does the fact of borrowing explain why an editor selected just this material, and placed it in just this context. What connection does disease and disability have with Deuteronomy's concept of true and false gods, and the ensuing demand for loyalty to one and mockery of the others?

I propose that the prominence of disability, combined with just these elements, constitutes not simply an historical potpourri, but a systematic ideological construction of true divinity and its elect worshippers as Normal. That is, the Normal construction of divinity also extends to the human worshippers. In the context of the covenant blessings and curses, health is not just a random good, and affliction a random evil. If health and ability are rewards for loyalty to Israel's God, then the Normal functions as reward for the Normal: worshippers acknowledge a god defined by sensate ability and freedom from physical incapacity, in return for which the god provides them with these Normal endowments. Conversely, the representation of idols as disabled—non-sensate and limited by physical matter, confined to their statues as it were—implicates the followers of idols in the disabilities of their gods. The exilic edition of Deuteronomy, in short, sets forth a Normal concept of divinity, and links its human Normal to the requirements of the divine Normal.

### Disability as Categorical Alterity

To what extent is this ideology distinctly Deuteronomic? Priestly literature also represents God as Normal, and makes some well-known Normal demands upon priests and sacrifices. However, Leviticus tends to treat disease and disability as impurity, linked to sin insofar as sin is a kind of impurity. But it seems to me that Priestly literature lacks Deuteronomy's sense of a plot: disease and disability, or other kinds of impurity, are states, but not narratives, for the Priestly literature. Compare, for instance, the representation of King Azariah/Uzziah's leprosy in DtH and Chronicles. DtH wants to give Azariah good grades, but has to explain his leprosy; thus it cites his failure to remove the high places in juxtaposition to his disease (2 Kgs 15:3–5). The priestly influenced Chronicler agrees with DtH's grading of Uzziah, but does not take over its explanation of his leprosy. Instead, we are told that, in his pride, he entered the Temple and performed an unauthorized sacrifice (2 Chr 26:16). This version has an attractive associative logic: spatial transgression leads to violation of the body's boundary, the skin. By contrast, DtH flounders to link a reasonably good king to a horrific punishment. Another cardinal difference emerges from this comparison: for DtH, disloyalty, with its whiff of idolatry, is the fatal error for which disease and disability are the penalties, but the Chronicler's God deals impurity for impurity.

Both Priestly and Deuteronomic literature, then, employ Normal representations of God, but the structures are not identical, and the human role in the Normal–Disabled dyad varies, as do the potentialities for sensory hierarchies and narrative enactments. Not all Normals are the same, nor are all Disabled others. Priestly literature represents God in strongly visual, spatial, and gestural terms. The Priestly Other is the blemished, the marred visual surface and the breached boundary. The divine Normal appears smooth, symmetrical, and unbreached. For Deuteronomic thought, the Other joins disloyalty, disease, and disability in a temporal-causal structure. The divine Normal does not appear, but speaks: the fiction of auditory representation undergirds Deuteronomy's construction of God as the real. In contrast, disability undergirds, even defines, the unreality of idols.

Chapter 3

FIGURES:
DISABILITY AS AESTHETIC DEVICE


And let thy Patriarches Desire
  (Those great Grandfathers of thy Church, which saw
    More in the cloud, than wee in fire,
  Whom Nature clear'd more, than us Grace and Law,
    And now in Heaven still pray, that wee
    May use our new helpes right,)
Be satisfy'd, and fructifie in me;
Let not my minde be blinder by more light
Nor Faith, by Reason added, lose her sight.

—John Donne, "The Litanie"[1]

What have the song of the morning stars, the treasures of the snow, the service of the unicorn, leviathan drawn on a hook, to do with Job's unmerited torments, with the motiveless malignity poured on his innocent head? Nothing whatever. To a moral challenge, God replies *aesthetically*, with a rhetorical display of his creative magnificence.

—George Steiner[2]

Priestly and Deuteronomic literature cast disability and ability into fairly static conceptual schemes, where the location and possession of disability can be clearly assigned. Nevertheless, these strata favor different sensory modes—the Priestly visualized body and the Deuteronomic auditory body—and this difference opens the breach into which time flows: unlike spatial arrangement, audition inherently contains temporality, for sound requires time for its existence and propagation. Narrative,

1. John Donne, *The Complete Poetry and Selected Prose of John Donne* (ed. Charles M. Coffin; New York: The Modern Library, 2001), 251.
2. George Steiner, "A Preface to the Hebrew Bible," in *No Passion Spent* (New Haven: Yale University Press, 1996), 72.

too, is inherently temporal, and in narrative, the potentialities of the disabled body expand. No longer merely a categorical marker, disability influences events and relationships. It becomes an aesthetic device, both through its propagation of narrative and through its potential for forming counter-narratives.

This chapter will examine disabled figures as they function in two major biblical narratives, Genesis and Job. Genesis is biblical prose narrative proper, a book of legends through which certain themes run. Disability frequently recurs in Genesis, to the extent that it should be regarded as a key motif. In addition, its relationship to the book's major themes of election and propagation is central, not peripheral. In fact, I shall argue that the through-narrative of Genesis depends on disability. More specifically, the related concepts of God's power and Israel's election depend, for their representations, on the representation of disability. As a partner to Genesis, Job may seem anomalous; it is wisdom literature, it combines prosaic and poetic sections in a dramatic framework, and it focuses on a single figure, for a brief period of fictive time. However, Job shares with Genesis a basic narrative in which disability plays a central role. Further, the book shows a sustained—sometimes subtle, sometimes overt—concern with mythologies of creation. Its dramatic portion allows the presentation of competing narratives, for the argument between Job and his friends can be seen as a contest of representations: Whose overall representation of the cosmos and its God is correct? Who, if anyone, is authorized to represent God? And how does the book as a whole provide a setting for Job's self-representation? Disability figures centrally in these questions. Finally, Genesis and Job would be on anybody's short-list for the canon within the canon, that is, those books that attract the most commentary and that tend to contribute excessively to various constructions of "biblical" worldviews or theologies on any subjects, and on disability in particular. Thus, careful examination and comparison of these works should yield significant insights into the role of disability in the Hebrew Bible. Although the history of interpretation lies beyond the scope of this study, I hope that a disability analysis of these books can encourage a more disability-aware critique of their deployment in biblical theologies as ways of placing disabled persons in Jewish and Christian history.[3]

---

3. Commentaries on both books are ripe for disability studies critiques of their ableist assumptions. Kerry Wynn's article "The Normate Hermeneutic and Interpretations of Disability within the Yahwistic Narratives," in *TAB*, 91–101, to be discussed more fully below, is a good model for future work in this vein.

## Narrative Prosthesis in Genesis

The theoretical work of Mitchell and Snyder, discussed in Chapter 1, provides an excellent tool for the analysis of disability in biblical narrative. In contrast to groups that are under-represented in literature, disabled persons, argue Mitchell and Snyder, are over-represented yet invisible. To explain this apparent paradox, they propose the concept of narrative prosthesis: "Our phrase *narrative prosthesis* is meant to indicate that disability has been used throughout history as a crutch upon which literary narratives lean for their representational power, disruptive potentiality, and analytical insight."[4] In other words, a narrative might depend on disability for its plot-initiating disruption and for its central metaphors. Regarding English and American literature, Mitchell and Snyder note a typical pattern of "repair": the disabled character introduces the anomaly that sets the plot in motion, and the narrative then uses elimination of the disability, or of the disabled character, for resolution.[5] One of their examples is Ahab in Melville's *Moby Dick*. His disabling injury gives him his mission to kill the whale that inflicted it. Had Ahab killed the whale but survived the encounter, the disability would have remained. Ahab's death removes the initial disruption in a way that his survival would not. According to Mitchell and Snyder, the wooden leg is not just Ahab's but the novel's prosthetic.[6] Disability's role in what used to be called a plot is then one locus for analysis.

Further, Mitchell and Snyder note two implications of this pattern. First, although disabled characters may be presented in a determinate, stereotypical way, the metaphorical presence of disability tends to destabilize the narrative's meanings;[7] the disabled cat gets out of the character bag and wreaks metaphorical havoc with the narrative's ostensible meanings. It is as if the prosthetic (disability) has a voice of its own, in conflict or counterpoint with the voices that speak from ability and tell readers to pay no attention to the crutch behind the curtain. Second, argue Mitchell and Snyder, "Disability inaugurates narrative, but narrative inevitably punishes its own prurient interests by overseeing the extermination of the object of its fascination."[8] The narrative-inducing disability must also be narratively effaced. These observations are based

4. Mitchell and Snyder, *Narrative Prosthesis*, 49 (emphasis original).
5. Ibid., 53–54.
6. Ibid., 47–64. Richard III in Shakespeare's plays is another one of their major examples.
7. Ibid., 50.
8. Ibid., 56–57

on a much later period of literature, and will need to be historically contextualized for the ancient Near East. On the other hand, their application to Genesis should help us discern whatever biblical influence may be present in the later pattern. From a strictly literary standpoint, we are looking first of all for disability as a means of narrative profluence—as an action-generating element. Beyond that, we shall also assess the broader metaphorical reach of these elements, any destabilizing features, and resolutions that attempt to efface or erase the initiating disabilities. As a means of exploring narrative prosthesis, I shall employ Avalos's sensory criticism to discern the implicit valuations that provide the opportunities for prosthesis, so to speak; where ideology generates or requires a weakness, it will also provide a support.

*Patriarchal Legends: Gendered Disability as Narrative Prosthesis*
As noted in Chapter 2, Priestly and Deuteronomic literature address themselves primarily to male bodies, and by extension, to male disability. Genesis, by contrast, shows a more systematic gendering of disability. To appreciate the gendered quality, it is important to recall the sense of "disability" that designates a body in a social environment. In ancient Israel, a woman's social value depended a great deal, if not entirely, on her ability to reproduce. Thus, as Avalos suggested, infertility was a disability for women.[9] The Hebrew Bible, in fact, rarely imagines that the male might be responsible for a couple's inability to conceive. The recurring appearance of barrenness as a threat to proper reproduction should not be news to anyone familiar with Genesis; the motif is hard to miss. Nevertheless, its quality as a disability has not been fully appreciated. Indeed, female infertility works together with a condition that Genesis presents as the distinctive male disability: blindness. Although some patriarchal cycles give greater prominence to one or the other condition, female infertility and male blindness together provide the narrative engine; without these, the patriarchal cycles would be episodic rather than integrally connected. Further, gendered disability plays a major role in the concept of second-son preference, which in turn provides one major component of the idea of election. Since election is a divine action, disability's role in it also has implications for the representation of God. Disability thus props up both the plot and at least two of its major themes.

---

9. Avalos, *Illness and Healthcare*, 331–34. See also, Neal H. Walls, "The Origins of the Disabled Body: Disability in Ancient Mesopotamia," in *TAB*, 13–30; his discussion of infertility is on p. 27.

*The Mythic Origin: Genesis 3 as Disabling Discourse.* Before turning to patriarchal legend, let us examine the biblical origin myth for disability in its broadest sense. For that, let us begin, not at the beginning, but near the end, of the composite myth. The act has been discovered, the excuses offered, and the divine judgment ensues. God first addresses the serpent (Gen 3:14): "Because you did this, cursed shall you be among all the land-animals and among all the beasts of the field; upon your belly shall you walk (תלך), and dust you shall eat all the days of your life."[10] Whether God's speech enacts the conditions stipulated against the three parties, or merely states results of which the actors were unaware, the curses upon the serpent, woman, and man point to new conditions. The verbs describing these conditions are imperfects that indicate future tense. The rhetoric has the tone of announcing something, not of referring to existing conditions. We have some description of pre-lapsarian human conditions to which the new situation contrasts; but how did the serpent "walk" before?[11]

The text does not say. Indeed, before this scene, only one term of description is used, "crafty" (ערום), with its evocation of "nakedness" (ערומים) in the preceding verse (2:25–3:1). Craftiness is operatively defined by the serpent's precocious rhetoric. He excels a peer group—the other wild animals—in cognitive skill, and shows a knack for intuiting weak points in Eve and in God. In short, he has exceptional abilities. Does the curse remove these abilities? The text does not say that God takes away the serpent's "craftiness." Going on one's belly and eating dust seem intended to humiliate, which could only be effective if the recipient understood his reduction in status. What might be called, inelegantly, a species-ableist maneuver seems to occur here: the equation of upright locomotion with status projects inherent goodness onto the human form. A non-human animal might not feel its own means of locomotion to be an insult. Nevertheless, the speech seems to presume that the serpent understands a changed condition, even as it neglects to provide the needed etiological myth for why serpents can no longer speak.[12] The presence or absence of speech does not seem that important

10. My translation.
11. In tagging the serpent's sentence as the etiological myth that it is, Coats jokes that anyone who wants to know why serpents crawl can look here. He does not say how one might find out how the serpent walked before. George W. Coats, *Genesis, with an Introduction to Narrative Literature* (Grand Rapids: Eerdmans, 1983), 56.
12. The term traditionally translated as "belly" occurs only in one other place in the MT: in Lev 11:42, on a list of prohibited meats, and also in relation to הלך as the "right" means of locomotion. Whatever walks on its belly is forbidden.

to me, for it does not stand out against the mythological background contrast of back-then and now. What matters is the serpent's intelligence, the implication of its continued presence, and the imposition of a form of locomotion to which the text attributes shame. Again, how did the serpent walk before? For a folkloric narrator or mythic poet, including the answer would take an easy aside. Why not answer it?

God's curse on the serpent is the first disabling in the Hebrew Bible. This should be clear even without a detail regarding the serpent's pre-lapsarian locomotion. Some ability has been taken away, by God, and this removal is characterized as a curse. Thus, whatever the serpent did before was better, in the text's terms of value. I suggest that the lack of detail on this point attempts to conceal the disabling quality of God's curses, just as so many things about God's character are half-concealed in this narrative. Absent the contrasting prior state, the speech in vv. 14–19 draws our attention to what the serpent, man, and woman did, and away from what God is doing. He is crippling them all.[13]

With the two human beings, the disabling is subtler. In the speech to the woman, God declares an increase in the pain of childbirth. Does this assume childbirth was painful before, and simply make it more difficult? Its unavoidable quality is emphasized in v. 16b. This speech does not contain a curse, probably because a curse on the source of life itself was too much even for a patriarchal writer. That would also explain why another obvious course of action is avoided: if the woman already has the (valued) ability to bear children, God could remove it. But then there would be no story. Instead, pain is added to something necessary.[14] Increased birth-pangs hamper the body in its former ability, and are thus disabling—as much as one would dare with a character who is the first mother. With the man, the term "curse" (ארר) returns, but is not directed at the man. The earth's fecundity is curtailed on account of the man's action (for which earth could not have been accountable) and in order to change *his* way of living. As with the woman, so with the earth: something natural gets much more difficult, which implies an earlier level of ability; and the ability is not completely removed. After all, complete removal for these entities would mean complete death for all. Death

13.  Danna Nolan Fewell and David M. Gunn, "Shifting the Blame: God in the Garden," in *Reading Bodies, Writing Bodies: Identity and the Book* (ed. Timothy K. Beal and David M. Gunn; London: Routledge, 1997), 16–33, analyze many of the shifts and distractions in this narrative. They do not mention the disabling quality of the curses, but their article influenced me toward this line of interpretation.

14.  For chronic pain, or pain unavoidably implicated in major life activities, see Susan Wendell, *The Rejected Body: Feminist Philosophical Reflections on Disability* (New York: Routledge, 1996), 170–72.

appears by dusty circumlocution at the end of God's speech to the man
(3:19). Dust (עָפָר) is what the serpent now eats: does the man become
food for serpents? Is death also a disabling, a removal of an earlier
ability, or was this always the case? This line does not contain a contrast
with a past situation, as did the other pronouncements. However that may
be, the Tree of Life implies a possibility—an ability—that is now closed
to humans.

The speech contains another interesting pairing of two against one:
the serpent and the woman are changed in their bodies. Some bodily
performance is removed or rendered far more difficult. In contrast, the
man's body is not changed. The earth, with which he will have to contend, is changed. This observation is valid whether or not death is a new
element, because the man's body, while alive, does not change, and the
serpent's and woman's do. Were they all to remain immortal (if they
are), or become so, this difference would still obtain. If they are all to die,
the difference remains. Death may introduce a time difference, a before-
and-after, but, as the author of Qohelet will later observe, it comes to all
equally. Yet the differential disablings are independent of death.

The intersection of these acts of cursing and disabling reveals a hierarchy of value. A combination of the cases, neglecting the death variable,
yields the following:

> Serpent—cursed; disabled in own body
> Woman—not cursed; disabled in own body
> Man—earth cursed on his account; not disabled

The cursing and the disabling have exempted precisely one thing: the
man's body. It will have to work harder for sustenance, but its ability to
do so has not changed. Further, neither human being is cursed, but the
serpent and the (non-culpable) earth are. This result is consistent with
Priestly source's assigned human role of subduing the earth and its
animal life (1:26). Finally, the serpent and the woman are differentially
disabled: in one case, an implied ability is removed, whereas in the other,
the obvious removal is suppressed in favor of a painful impediment to
the function. Further, the hierarchy thus established does not just add
incidental features to fully defined beings; the results are role-defining.

They are also plot-generating. Genesis as a whole contains numerous
references to bodily impairments and disease. A narrow view of bodily
impairment, for example, as just blindness, deafness, or lameness, or some
other specifically named disability, will fail to capture the full pattern.
However, an understanding of disability as bodily impairment in the
context of social environment reveals that female infertility, seldom
viewed as a disability in modern post-industrial societies, *is* the defining

female disability in the Hebrew Bible (and in other ancient Near Eastern literature). Nor are male disabilities in Genesis random: blindness seems to be the defining one. Further, male blindness and female infertility tend to occur together or to intersect in a highly specific way, as a threat to progeny—and not to human progeny in general, but only to the kind of progeny backed by God, so to speak. I shall flesh out this thesis with detailed discussion of passages, but it bears mention at the outset that the pattern raises the question, why should disability threaten this God-sanctioned procreation?

*The Abraham Cycle.* In the Abraham cycle, female infertility may be the most prominent disability motif, and a prominent motif in any reckoning. In a more sensory-critical and less obvious vein, Abraham shows an uncanny visuality at key moments; thus male sightedness is the partner of female infertility in this portion of the patriarchal narratives. Abraham's visual ability provides a subtle contrast to Isaac's blindness, and together, these set up the nuanced treatment of male vision and its deficits.

Following upon the Tower of Babel, Gen 11:10–32 is the genealogy from Noah's son Shem to Abram. The passage separates primordial myth and legend from the patriarchal cycles. Among this list of begots, very few editorial remarks supplement the list, and no female names appear until those of Abram's and his brother Nahor's wives. At that point, the two women are named, and the narrator makes a terse remark on Sarai's infertility (11:30).[15] The simple statement, embedded as it is in a list, nevertheless provides a crucial piece of information for the narrative that is about to resume.

The beginning of the narrative does not explicitly take up barrenness. At the beginning of Gen 12, Abram is told to leave Haran and continue to Canaan (an earlier family journey that seems to have been aborted for unstated reasons; see Gen 11:31–32). Along with this order, God promises Abram that he will father a great nation, and that his descendants will inherit the land where he has just moved (12:1–7). Abram never speaks in response to these divine speeches; he simply acts, and mainly, he moves. Genesis 12:4 notes his age during this migration, but the absence of offspring is not mentioned yet. Thus, the narrator provides, parenthetically, additional information that draws attention to the lack of procreation, which contrasts sharply with God's references to future offspring.

15. Coats notes the importance of this brief remark, without which the irony of ch. 12 cannot occur. Coats, *Genesis*, 107.

Immediately after this passage, the first of the triplets about a patriarchal sojourn in Egypt occurs. The source-critical use of the triplets is well-known, and not relevant to this project. However, Biddle's analysis of the roots related to the guilt and the sin offering demonstrates that these triplets all pertain to the means by which the patriarch in question will be a blessing to the nations.[16] Although he does not examine the disease and disability motifs at any length, their presence fits well with Biddle's contention that each story poses the possibility of another nation profaning something sacred;[17] appropriate bodily harm occurs, as if automatically, in two of the doublets, and is mentioned as a possibility just avoided in the third. The two versions in the Abraham cycle interweave Abram/Abraham's domestic story in which Sarai/Sarah's barrenness figures explicitly, and both establish a connection between Sarai/Sarah and physical illness or infertility.[18]

In the first version, which follows Abram's migration into Canaan, the couple sojourns in Egypt on account of famine. Sarai's beauty provides both the warrant for the lie (12:11) and the occasion for Pharaoh's marriage to her (12:14, 19). But Sarai, or more precisely, the (potential) transgression of her, comes with God's plagues (נגעים, 12:17). It goes without saying—and in fact hovers unstated over this pericope—that Abram cannot father offspring if his wife has been re-married to Pharaoh. In short, bodily features (Sarai's great beauty) cause the threat to Abram's reproductive potential, and bodily disease (Pharaoh's household) removes the threat and restores the couple to each other.

The second version, in ch. 20, occurs after the first explicit promise of offspring to Sarah (Gen 17), but before she conceives Isaac. This placement is fraught with implication. Abraham is sojourning in Gerar after the Sodom and Gomorrah episode, and the couple again conceal their marriage. With no mention of Sarah's attractiveness, Abimelech, the local king, takes Sarah as his wife. Here, the narrator takes pains to show that Abimelech did not consummate this marriage: there is a direct reports that he did not (20:4), God warns him immediately (20:3), and a conversation between Abimelech and God treats the matter. That con-

16. Mark E. Biddle, "The 'Endangered Ancestress' and Blessing for the Nations," *JBL* 109, no. 4 (1990): 599–611.
17. Ibid., 606.
18. Susan Niditch's delightful folkloric analysis nevertheless misses this point. She notices theological differences among the three variants, and refers to the God of Gen 12 as just a "plague-sender." But that divine threat lurks in all of the stories. Susan Niditch, *Underdogs and Tricksters: A Prelude to Biblical Folklore* (San Francisco: Harper & Row, 1987), esp. Chapter 2, "The Three Wife-Sister Tales of Genesis," 23–69. The remarks about God and plagues are on p. 63.

versation adds divine warrant to Abimelech's own claim that he did not touch the woman. Abimelech and Abraham then discuss the situation, with Abraham offering an explanation for the deception, and Abimelech offering property as a settlement. Apparently, nothing else needs to be done, for God had threatened death to all in the household (20:3, 7). Only at the conclusion does the narrator add that God healed Abimelech and his household, where God had made the women infertile (20:17–18). The placement is clumsy: Abimelech was trying to avoid a death threat, not infertility, which was not mentioned earlier. Further, the body of the narrative contains clear temporal cues that suggest, but not decisively, a single day time-frame. It is not clear how much time passes between v. 2b, when Sarah arrives in the household, and v. 3, when Abimelech has his dream. The conversation with Abraham occurs the morning after the dream (20:8). Indeed, without the closing reference to widespread infertility, which would take some time to be noticed, there would be little reason to think the story occurs in more than a single day. In any case, this doublet, like the first, poses a threat to *Abraham's* having a child *by Sarah*; the new details in the promises of Gen 17 seem to draw the newly specific threat. They also add to the association between Sarah and physical ailment generally—and infertility specifically. In spite of the narrator's insistence that Abimelech had no sexual relations with Sarah, an aura of protesting too much hangs over this segment; Sarah conceives in the verse following this episode's conclusion.

Having noted these interwoven doublets that depict Sarah's effect on the fertility of others, let us turn to Sarah's own barrenness. Abram's tale begins in Gen 12, but the narrator implies his lack of children by omission; none are mentioned. The first explicit mention comes in Gen 15, one of the Abram's theophanies. Abram has a vision (מחזה, 15:1a) that opens with a divine promise of reward (15:1b). Abram's reply links the ideas of reward and offspring (15:2). Thus, reward without fertility is meaningless, because the inheritance goes to others. While the text does not quite equate reward and offspring, it does make the former conditional upon the latter. Further, Abram lays the responsibility for his childlessness on God (15:3). The divine response that follows asserts that Abram will be the biological father of these heirs (15:4). Who shall be the mother of this heir is not stated. The passage moves on to a discussion of the land promise, including the *ex post facto* allusion to enslavement in Egypt.

The episodes in ch. 16 revolve around Abram's family life. Here, for the first time since the genealogy in Gen 11, the narrator explicitly states Sarai's childlessness (16:1a). This notice initiates a sequence of action.

Verse 16:1b paratactically introduces Hagar, as if these two data—
Sarai's childlessness and Hagar's presence in the household—contain the
rest of the mini-plot. Sarai proposes that Hagar provide them with a
child, and Abram assents. I do not think either character is fleshed out so
fully that one can overly individualize their approaches to the situation.
Rather, the passage provides a poignant window into the social situation
of the barren woman, in its depiction of the post-conception conflict
between the two women. Hagar views her pregnancy as a chance to rise,
socially; the fertile woman outranks the barren one. In response, Sarai
asserts the power of the slaveholder over the slave. Both Abram and God
uphold the propriety of Sarai's harshness toward Hagar, even as God
promises the runaway many descendents.

This domestic struggle is framed by two theophanies. The second, in
Gen 17, opens with an appearance and a speech to Abram. This divine
speech, like the previous ones, contains the elements of promised offspring and land. It adds the concept of a covenant and a re-naming.
Genesis 17:9–14 describes the circumcisions of all males in the household as a sign of the covenant. If readers are to imagine how Abraham
takes in all this new information, we infer that he is thinking about Ishmael first of all. Indeed, when he carries out these instructions, Ishmael is
mentioned first, and is the only person besides Abraham mentioned by
name (17:23). Without a pause long enough for Abraham to speak or
question, God finally specifies the matriarch (17:15–16). If we consider
these as speech acts, one would call them initiations, and specifically,
patriarch- or matriarch-making speeches. Abraham has already received
several patriarch-making speeches and performed acknowledging rituals (Gen 15), but this is the first and only matriarch-making speech
for Sarah.[19] In addition to its commandment of circumcision, then, this
theophany creates a matriarch.

The matriarch-making quality of Gen 17:15–16 prompts one to
compare the angel's speech to Hagar (16:9–12). Here, the elements of
the angel's speech are as follows: command to return to the household;
promise to increase offspring; notice of existing pregnancy; naming
command and promise to Ishmael. At the time of this encounter, Hagar is
already pregnant; that is, no divine speech about her or Ishmael preceded
the conception. With Sarah, the order is reversed: divine speech first,
including promise of numerous descendants, and then conception. Nor is
Hagar barren. Thus, the narrative depicts two parallel ways of conceiving, one ordinary and blessed *ex post facto*, and the other extraordinary

---

19. I regard the statements by the mysterious men in Gen 18 as time-frame
predictions, not initiations.

and blessed before the (narrative) fact. The former assumes fertility as the Normal female ability, and draws attention to its high social value (16:4–6). The latter means of propagation requires both the element of disability—Sarah's barrenness and her barrenness-inducing effect on other households—and the element of divine speech as the key inducement to conception. Finally, only the latter way provides for the "right" offspring, although the text does not depict the ordinary means as "wrong." On the contrary, Abraham's actions in Gen 16 are probably an attempt to fulfill his part of the deal in ch. 15. He does not know until ch. 17 that God wants a bigger hand in the propagation.

Now, one way of viewing this sequence of events would be to see God as the powerful healer, but in order to be that, God needs human disability—here, female infertility—as a narrative prosthesis. Put another way, the text requires human disability in order to make its point about God's power. Its representation of God's power rests on the back of an infertile woman. So does the plot. Let us imagine what the story could be without the element of Sarai's barrenness. Abram migrates from place to place. If Sarai is fertile, he has children by her and perhaps also some children by concubines or additional wives. The oldest son probably inherits, although perhaps the son of the best-loved wife would. And God keeps promising land in the distant future. Two important observations emerge from this counterfactual narrative. First, it is episodic; the episodes have no integral links between them. There is no reason to take a concubine, no reason for her to run away, no blessing on the first son, no need for divine speeches to make patriarchs or matriarchs. The Abraham cycle becomes an itinerary with stops of varying interest, rather like Twain's *Huckleberry Finn* (and often as bizarre, if less humorous). Second, God's role then includes two functions, telling Abraham where to go next (an ancient GPS voice), and promising land—a promise that is never delivered on during the Abraham cycle. It should be clear just how much the female disability of infertility is doing for this narrative and its character named God. Sarai's infertility provides the major occasion for God to come through on a promise to Abraham during Abraham's lifetime. Without this element, God would seem rather ineffectual—all words and little action. Abraham, in turn, would have children or not, by his first wife or not, like other men do or do not.

Incidentally, the episode of Sodom and Gomorrah contains a few variations on the disability theme, variations that throw the main themes into sharper relief. The tale is not essential to the Israelite patriarchal plot, but it contains an interesting linkage of male blindness with a threat to "proper" propagation. In Gen 19:4–11, the townspeople surround

Lot's house and demand that he turn over the visitors for rape. Lot offers his virgin daughters to buy them off. At that point, the visitors (angels) pull him in and strike the crowd with a "blinding light" (סנוורים, 19:11). Apparently, the effect is temporary and tactical: the assailants cannot see the entrance into which they would break. Note the timing of the angelic intervention, not at the beginning of the assault, but only after Lot has offered his daughters. These daughters then later mate with their father when the latter is drunk out of his wits (19:33–35). The temporary blinding, then, preserves the *daughters* for this later ruse and role; the angels are not protecting themselves (they could have done that before Lot offered the girls), although the impressive means by which they ward off a threat to Lot's daughters indicate that they were quite capable of taking care of themselves in a fight, if it came to that. Further, by "proper" reproduction, I do not mean anything as simple as other-sex versus same-sex. The daughters are preserved virgins not to couple with just any man, but specifically with their father, and specifically to bring about the patriarchs of the Moabites and Ammonites. This tale is a patriarchal narrative of two non-Israelite peoples, in which temporary disability plays a protective role. Genesis 19 differs from the Abraham and Isaac cycles in that the disability attaches to a third party, the one excluded from a role, whereas for the Israelite patriarchs, female infertility and male blindness attach to the patriarchs and matriarchs themselves.

*The Isaac Cycle: Who Needs to See?* Let us turn, then, to that patriarch of blindness, Isaac. Commentators have focused on the ostensible onset of blindness and, to a lesser extent, on its metaphorical role earlier in the cycle. Here, Kerry Wynn has provided a useful critique of what he terms the "normate hermeneutic" operating in contemporary interpretations of Isaac.[20] Wynn employs the term "normate" from Garland Thomson's work; as mentioned above, it indicates an ideological construction of a "right" body and thus entails a variety of "wrong" bodies. With respect to biblical interpretations, Wynn elaborates thus: "The 'normate hermeneutic' is the means by which scripture is interpreted so that it complies with and reinforces the socially constructed norms. This hermeneutic imposes a society's interpretation of disability on the text without due consideration to the text itself."[21] It is, in other words, a form of eisegesis, a way of reading attitudes into the text rather than asking the prior question whether they are really there. With this in mind, Wynn examines

---

20. Wynn, "Normate Hermeneutic."
21. Ibid., 92.

both Isaac's blindness and Jacob's limp; I shall deal with the latter briefly below. Regarding Isaac, Wynn argues convincingly that Isaac's blindness never diminishes his patriarchal role. Instead, the statuses of Rebekah, Esau, and Jacob remain entirely dependent on Isaac's valuation of them. Their trickster stratagem indicates Isaac's greater power, not his vulnerability, for the most powerful party would not resort to tricks:

> It is the status of Jacob and Esau that is at stake. The status of Isaac as patriarch and his power to grant the blessing are never brought into question in light of his age or his blindness... That Rebekah and Jacob disable Isaac through dishonesty in accommodations does not reflect on the ability of Isaac but upon Rebekah and Jacob. When the text of Genesis 27 is freed from the normate hermeneutic and examined in light of what it actually says and in light of the historical context of its writing, a totally different picture of the patriarch appears. We must reject the traditional Isaac as a "powerless dependent" for Isaac, the "powerful patriarch" with all the sexist implications that come with this patriarchal role.[22]

I agree substantially with Wynn's conclusion that Isaac with his visual impairment remains quite able, relative to the others. However, in critiquing scholars who associate age-related blindness with death and weakness,[23] Wynn places more emphasis than I think necessary on the late onset of Isaac's blindness and on its incidental quality relative to the rest of his life. If we attend to representational questions, especially to how the senses characterize the figures, we find that sight and sightlessness play important rather than incidental roles in the depiction of a forceful patriarchal figure.

I begin with a literal and perhaps pedestrian question: when does Isaac lose his sight? The first explicit mention of visual impairment occurs in Gen 27:1. Instead of asking when Isaac stops seeing, I suggest that we ask, "When does Isaac see?" Then, tantalizing hints appear much earlier, perhaps as literary foreshadowing, or perhaps as representation of early-onset, progressive visual impairment. This question might not be fruitful if the narrative simply assumed sight for all of the characters. However, throughout the Isaac cycle, the narrator continually draws attention to other characters' sight and their uses of it, a kind of attention from which Isaac is strangely exempt. The verb ראה can be regarded as a *leitwort*, in Alter's sense: a recurring word that expresses a central motif or idea.[24] In

22. Ibid., 96.
23. This interpretation appears most prominently in his critique of Niditch; ibid., 93–94.
24. Robert Alter, *The Art of Biblical Narrative* (New York: Basic, 1981), 92–93.

this case, it also characterizes, for everyone around Isaac seems to take in the most important information by sight, whereas in the one sentence that predicates sight of Isaac, he does not see the important thing (and apparently does not need to). This contrast establishes a subtle difference between Isaac and others, a difference which becomes more overt as he ages.

Isaac first appears at birth and in childhood, in Gen 21. The birth pericope emphasizes the aural-oral modes for all figures. God does as he said and spoke (21:1); Sarah bears at the spoken time (21:2); and Abraham adheres to the earlier spoken command of circumcision on the eighth day (21:3). This sequence builds up to Sarah's highly auditory naming statement (21:6):

צחק עשה לי אלהים כל־השמע יצחק־לי

God made laughter for me; all who hear will laugh with me.[25]

The word order places "laughter" and "those who hear" in grammatical parallelism, thus placing the most auditory element, in nominal forms, first in the sentence. That Isaac's name comes from the root meaning "to laugh" has been well noted. As for Isaac in childhood, the narrator does not yet depict him seeing, or even doing, anything. Nevertheless, sensory gradients surround him. His naming emphasizes hearing, and the familial separation in which he figures depends on a certain sight: Sarah sees (ותרא) Ishmael "playing" (21:9)[26] and insists that he and Hagar go. Such a simple narrative report might easily slip under awareness, unless we realize that this provocation could come in any number of ways, through various sensory media, or without reference to the senses. Even earlier, the conflict between the women, which could be rendered in dialogue or competition for affection, is cast in highly sighted terms (Gen 16:4):

ותרא כי הרתה ותקל גברתה בעיניה

She saw that she had conceived, and her mistress was diminished in her eyes.[27]

Sarai's complaint to Abram (16:5) repeats both terms. The narrative thus prepares for the final break to come through Sarah's vision. Isaac is not even the object of sight, at least not directly; nevertheless, he, even as an absence or a possibility, is a focal point. In any case, the representation

25. My translation.
26. That the verse plays on Isaac's name is well-noted. Joel Kaminsky lists the possibilities in "Humor and the Theology of Hope: Isaac as Humorous Figure," *Interpretation* (October 2000): 363–75 (366).
27. My translation; many translators replace the visual terms with abstractions.

of Isaac's infancy and early life features auditory description and perception for him, while vision takes center stage in Ishmael's exit.[28] With respect to both boys, Sarah's perceptions and sensory modes—auditory for Isaac, visual for Ishmael—carry great weight.

Isaac next appears in the tortuous episode of Gen 22. To be sure, the sacrifice of Isaac does not say anything explicit about Isaac's vision. However, it does use the verb to see (ראה) as an important means of characterization for both Abraham and God.[29] The initial divine communication is oral-auditory, and a sequence of swift actions follows it. Moriah emerges in Abraham's vision (22:4), yet the verb never occurs to describe Isaac's perceptions. Isaac uses the demonstrative particle (הנה) to indicate their equipment, which he might be aware of through touch or through hearing the preparations. Abraham's reply strangely emphasizes visuality (אלהים יראה־לו, 22:8). There are other ways of expressing this idea in Hebrew, and indeed, English translations vary on how they render "to see" in this passage.[30] So far, Abraham sees and God sees; but does Isaac see anything? Commentators have long noticed the lack of response from Isaac as he is bound to the altar, even as his father raises the knife to kill him. Nor does the narrator disclose any of Isaac's perceptions, tactile, auditory, or olfactory. A sequence of audition–vision, much like the initial one, interrupts the action: a voice speaks, and Abraham responds in speech, and then he looks up (22:13a) and sees the ram. If all this seeing were not enough to draw our attention, the narrator has Abraham name the place "Adonai-Yireh," literally, "YHWH will see"—his response to Isaac in 22:8, saving only the change of divine name. In contrast to Gen 15, where the perceptual mode is visionary (חזן) rather than merely visual (ראה), this passage resorts constantly to the ordinary term for human sight. Further, these terms are predicated of Abraham and God, but never of Isaac. Sight is a sensory mode of communication that God and Abraham share, and in which Isaac does not participate. I do not mean to suggest that this passage provides evidence that Isaac is already blind; it does not, or at least, not clearly. Instead, my point is that vision is absent from the entire characterization of Isaac: not only does the narrator omit seeing for him, while emphasizing it for the other key parties, but Isaac never responds to any information that he could not have obtained just as well without vision, and he never behaves in a way

28. Hagar's flight continues the motif (Gen 21:16–19).

29. Westermann observes the importance of the sight motif for Abraham, but does not include Isaac in his analysis of it. Claus Westermann, *Genesis* (trans. David E. Green; Edinburgh: T. & T. Clark, 1987), 161–62.

30. The NRSV translation of this verse avoids concrete terms for sight.

that requires sight. This feature would not even be noticeable, except for the narrator's frequent representation of sight for other characters, and for an interpreter willing to withhold the Normal assumption of universal vision and allow the text to say how a character perceives his world. Perhaps the legendary stock imagined a younger, sighted Isaac; a later passage, to be discussed below, depicts Isaac seeing something, although not very clearly. The Genesis narrative, however, makes him representationally blind as soon as he is an agent of action, rather than just the object of his parents' actions.

The narrative represents the adult Isaac as sighted, yet in a curiously muted way in comparison to his highly visual father and to others around him. First of all, the account of Isaac's marriage to Rebekah plays with sight. Abraham sends a servant to obtain a daughter-in-law from his kinsmen (24:1–9), in an opening scene that marks Isaac as stationary and the prospective wife as mobile. The land promise provides the narrator's stated rationale, and perhaps also the unstated reason why Abraham does not send Isaac to select his own wife. Kaminsky, along with others, takes this lack of mobility to indicate Isaac's passivity, perhaps even a cognitive impairment.[31] Poor vision at an early age could also explain Abraham's use of a servant for this task; as mentioned in the introduction, the Hebrew Bible often regards blindness as a mobility impairment. In any case, on arrival, the servant prays for an auditory sign, a word omen, and thereby meets Rebekah at the well. Rebekah, a great beauty, appears to the servant and the reader simultaneously (24:16). They exchange the stipulated words, as the servant sustains his gaze upon her (24:21). After the introductions, they return to her home, and once again, a visual cue alerts a character, here Laban, to important information: he sees the nose-ring and arm-bands Rebekah now wears (24:30). The servant then recites his errand, closely following Abraham's direct discourse, and closely rehearsing the recent encounter, except that he omits his observation of the girl's beauty. Her family tersely agrees to the marriage, and with one attempted delay, Rebekah and the servant depart. The narrator then returns to Isaac, who camps and will later settle at Beer-Lahai-Roi, or "Well of the Living One Who Sees Me" (24:62; 25:11). But who sees whom? When Isaac and Rebekah first encounter each other, an interesting visual asymmetry occurs. The same distance separates Isaac and Rebekah from each other when Isaac raises his eyes and sees the camels,

31. Kaminisky, "Humor," 368. Although insightful in many ways, Kaminsky's willingness to denigrate Isaac's mental capacities begs for a disability critique. Isaac's successful negotiations with other ethnic groups and the great wealth he accumulates would argue against such an interpretation.

whereas Rebekah raises hers and sees Isaac (24:63–64).[32] The earlier
description of her beauty and of a new male's reaction to her only
emphasize what Isaac does not see: the beautiful woman who shall be
his wife. The first words between the two are not narrated, yet their relationship begins with a lack of visual reciprocity. In the marriage arrange-
ments, then, we have a woman so visually striking that men react strongly.
Her appearance signals her unmarried state to the servant, and her change
of situation to her brother. At the couple's first sight of each other, what
they see or notice is asymmetrical. Indeed, Isaac is the first male in this
narrative who does not respond visually to Rebekah. Actions (bring,
take) and then emotions (love, comfort) characterize his response. Either
his visual impairment has already begun, or he simply does not respond
strongly to her beauty. Then they settle by the Well of the Living One
Who Sees Me. This is not to read any particular valuation into Isaac's
visual capacities; I simply observe that, in various subtle ways that betray
a pattern, the narrator marks Isaac as different from the others because he
does not (can no longer?) rely on vision. Yet he prospers, to the effect
that sight begins to look like a crutch that others need and Isaac does not.

Unlike other patriarchal couples, Isaac and Rebekah directly join male
blindness and female infertility. If my interpretation above is convincing,
then Isaac's visual impairment emerges first. After the interlude of
Abraham's death and some brief genealogies, the narrative begins again
with Isaac, and then introduces Rebekah's barrenness (25:21). Compared
to Sarah's situation, the resolution comes quickly: she conceives twins
and has a difficult pregnancy. Coats observes that the terminology here
indicates response to a petition, not the proper term for healing.[33] The
question of inheritance or blessing then develops between Esau and
Jacob, fraternal twins. Isaac and Rebekah have no other children, nor
would more children be necessary. Perhaps the relative simplicity here,
compared to the familial complications of Sarah's barrenness, is a matter
of narrative weighting. Either motif, female infertility or male blindness,
is sufficient to generate the threat-to-propagation plot; with both together,
full elaboration would become cumbersome and melodramatic.

The episodes in Gen 26, although not directly about impairments or
disabilities, contain some variations on the Isaac themes. During a famine,
the couple must move around and encounter threats and opportunities.
Their initial displacement to Gerar begins with an apparent triplet to

---

32. Kaminsky's suggestion that she sees him urinating or defecating is both
possible and funny (ibid., 369). The asymmetry in their visual acuity remains the
case.

33. Coats, *Genesis*, 184: עתר rather than רפה.

accompany the Abram/Abraham doublet of the "She's my sister" motif. As with doublets and triplets, the differences leap to the foreground. First of all, Rebekah is already a mother by Isaac, so the potential for another marriage would threaten the family unit, but not Isaac's status as progenitor. Second, and also unlike the Abraham doublet, the narrator does not report any premeditation to the lie. It comes across as an on-the-spot dodge to a problematic question (26:7). Finally, unlike Sarah, Rebekah is not taken into anyone's house as a new wife. Abimelech's scolding of Isaac points to a possible, not actual, effect of his lie (26:10). This much is easy to see. However, the crucial differentiating details pertain to sight. In Gen 12, Abram knows that Sarai is beautiful; Pharaoh's courtiers see her beauty and recommend her; plagues then occur. In Gen 20, neither Abraham nor his hosts (nor the narrator) mention Sarah's beauty, but God warns Abimelech in a dream, and he quickly remedies the situation. One could call this version the sight-less one, for it does not refer to seeing at all, much less the seeing of anything important. Instead, it favors the auditory and tactile, emphasizing what was heard or not, touched or not (20:3–7).

The Isaac–Rebekah version contains two visual details. First, Isaac knows that his wife is beautiful (26:7). Yet the narrator never mentions how Isaac came to this opinion. Visually impaired people do have some concepts of beauty and can notice how others react differently to different people, and form is tactilely perceptible. Might the narrator be relying on the assumptions of an implied sighted reader? Although possible, such a conjecture would make it difficult to explain the use of terms for sight in the differential characterization of Isaac relative to others. With that in mind, it seems more likely that Isaac has a progressive visual impairment and has formed this opinion primarily through other senses. As for the second visual detail, on it hangs the mini-plot: Abimelech looks out of a window and sees the couple apparently engaged in love-making (26:8). Thus, the key piece of information reaches the key player through vision, a sense underlined, as it were, by the double terms for it, just as the double use of the root צחק underlines Isaac's relationship to Rebekah. Abimelech's sight saves his people from the plagues, infertility, and risk of death that a reader, recognizing the parallel accounts, would expect. Finally, Isaac's ruse leads to strong protection for them both: bothering Isaac and Rebekah becomes, by royal pronouncement, a capital crime. In contrast to his parents, who escape unscathed and with some compensatory gifts, Isaac is spectacularly successful, gaining wealth in land, livestock, and water resources until the Philistines demand that he separate from them.

The dispute over wells in the latter half of ch. 26 sustains this narrative contrast between others who see the key piece of information, and Isaac who does not, or does not need to. Isaac and his servants have been digging wells, which the Philistines then claim. At last, his household seems to have undisputed possession of a well at Beer-Sheba. When Abimelech comes with an entourage to discuss the wells, he tells Isaac that his people now "see" that God provides for Isaac (26:27–28). But this pericope, like the others, does not represent Isaac seeing anything.[34] Isaac knows what he knows without seeing anything; the Philistines see, finally and forcefully enough for the double helping of an infinite absolute and a main verb. As in other Isaac episodes, others see or need to see in order to understand Isaac, but he has no reciprocal need.

In the entire Isaac cycle, I find only one usage that implicates Isaac in vision. His dealings with the Philistines in ch. 26 are bracketed by two theophanies. Both use the niphal of ראה in identical constructions (26:2; cf. 26:24). This construction occurs numerous times in Genesis and elsewhere to describe a theophany.[35] Semantically, the term carries an obvious sense of making oneself visible to another. Sometimes, a contextual cue establishes a visual theophany, whether or not "appear" depicts the divine action. For instance, when Jacob wrestles with the angel, no one "appears," but Jacob exclaims in the end that he has seen God face to face (32:31). Abram's theophany in Gen 12 highlights visual description without using this verb. The question, then, is whether the text represents Isaac seeing God. After all, even before Gen 27, Isaac's vision is an odd thing, and so are theophanies. That being the case, in the absence of an additional cue similar to Jacob's place-naming statement, I do not think that these two occurrences can establish a fully sighted Isaac.

At last, we come to the fully blind Isaac of Gen 27. The word choice suggests a progressive condition that has reached a significant degree of impairment (27:1):

ויהי כי־זקן יצחק ותכהין עיניו מראת

When Isaac was old and his eyes were dim so that he could not see. (NRSV)

---

34. Many English translations render the adversative *waw* as "seeing that." Although this accurately captures the meaning in idiomatic English, a *waw* expressing an idea is not enough to count as Isaac seeing something. In fact, this English expression has the unfortunate effect of representing Isaac and the Philistines as sharing a sensory modality and coming to an accommodation through it, when the Hebrew contains no such suggestion.

35. Divine appearance to Abram/Abraham at Gen 12:7 (twice); 17:1; 18:1; to Jacob/Israel, Gen 35:1.

Isaac believes that he may die soon and wants to bless Esau; Rebekah contrives the ruse so that Jacob obtains the blessing. Coats observes a sensory framing in the first part: Isaac's request to Esau emphasizes taste, Rebekah overhears, and her plan then seizes upon taste.[36] Before this big deception scene, the narrator has incorporated some telling characterization. The passage at 25:27–34 established the different favoritisms of each parent, and the different habits of each son. There, Jacob tricks Esau out of his birthright without any parental involvement. Then, at the end of the Gerar episode, the narrator notes Esau's marriage to two Hittite women, a situation that displeases both parents (26:34–35). In fact, this notice immediately precedes the blessing of Jacob. When his younger son enters the room, Isaac seems skeptical of the son's identity. He considers the voice, the hairiness, and the smell—auditory, tactile, and olfactory modes—and notes the disagreement between sound and touch (27:22). The request of a kiss is probably an attempt to resolve this discrepancy: the scent apparently convinces (27:27), and Jacob receives the blessing. Have Rebekah and Jacob taken advantage of a blind man, or is something else going on?

Wynn forcefully argues that Isaac remains the most powerful player in this domestic drama,[37] and I concur. The passive-Isaac line of interpretation fails to account for too much in the Isaac cycle. Here, Isaac is quite active in ordering Jacob about and testing his claims; he just makes the wrong inference. Yet he blesses the "right" son. Isaac's inability to see does not threaten Genesis's narrative of proper propagation, it ensures it. Further, an oracle during pregnancy has told Rebekah that the younger son was the important one (Gen 25:23), although the narrator does not tell whether she shares this information with Isaac. Instead, patriarchal blindness parallels matriarchal barrenness quite closely, for both bypass the expected in favor of the "right" son. (By "right," I mean Genesis's ideological concern with securing a particular descent, a thread through the generations that leads to the Israelite people.) The narrative uses this displacement away from human agency and ordinary means in order to represent divine agency and extraordinary means.

One more non-Normal hermeneutical move yields further insight. If we resist the distraction of how Isaac can get along in his competitive family without sight, we might ask instead, does anybody else see anything? This question leads to an interesting contrast with Isaac's family of origin, for his own family seems to be highly auditory. Rebekah's and

36. Coats, *Genesis*, 203.
37. Wynn, "Normate Hermeneutic," 95.

Jacob's conniving is highly auditory: Rebekah overhears Isaac's instructions to Esau (27:5), she mentions this mode of discovery again to Jacob (27:6), and she commands him to hear (27:8). The audiocentricity here is more than an operating assumption that direct discourse implies hearing; the verb occurs three times in four verses, when it is not necessary. Hurried action follows, but sight is not attributed to either of them. This is not to say that they are blind, but rather than they get all of their information and perform all of their activities without sight providing the important means of knowledge or action. In the next scene, Isaac is the point-of-view character: the narrator follows his attempts to determine his son's identity, but we do not get to see Isaac through Jacob's eyes. Instead, we hear, touch, and smell Jacob with Isaac's other senses. In scene three, Esau arrives too late. When he declares himself, Isaac reacts with violent convulsions (27:33). Trembling can be visual or visceral, depending on point of view. But the narrator reports Isaac's trembling to the reader; he does not show Esau seeing it or addressing it in any way. After Isaac blurts out what has just happened, Esau hears the words (27:34) and sobs violently (the construction grammatically parallels Isaac's trembling). The pair come across as loud and heart-wrenching, but not as visualized figures. The second-best blessing follows as denouement, and Esau leaves with a grudge against his brother. In representational terms, no one has seen anything.

In the aftermath, Rebekah gets a report of Esau's intent to kill Jacob, and she again advises her favorite in audiocentric terms (27:43). No one tells Isaac of this result. Instead, Rebekah offers to Isaac the pretext that Jacob should not marry a Hittite woman. She does not say "as Esau did," but she does not have to: Isaac agrees without argument. Recall that the narrator had these two in agreement about Esau's selection of wives. One wonders whether Rebekah's pretext for Jacob's flight was also her main reason for orchestrating Jacob's receipt of the blessing. In any case, Esau seems to draw this inference. The whole episode of the misplaced blessing and family break-up concludes with the first visual reference since the opening statement of Isaac's blindness: Esau "sees" that Jacob has left with another blessing, and further "sees" that his Canaanite wives did not suit his parents (וַיַּרְא both times, Gen 28:6–8). So he marries one of Ishmael's daughters, as if that could help things now. As with the audiocentric passages between Rebekah and Jacob, the passage has an over-determined quality. This idea could be expressed without the verb "to see," but instead we have it gratuitously doubled, a lone pair in a passage where no one else saw because no one else needed to see. Esau did not lose his paternal blessing because of Isaac's blindness; he lost it

because of his own. Both blindnesses, the physical and the representational, form the pathway through which "right" propagation is secured
(here, against the Hittites). Sight in its metaphorical sense as knowledge
occurs too late to change the course of action—of election. This is the
case for both Esau and Isaac, who, once fully informed, again blessed
Jacob (28:1–4).

*The Jacob Cycle*
The interlocking motifs of sightedness/blindness and barrenness continue
through the Jacob cycle, although they may be less apparent than other
motifs, for example, the trickster tricked, impressive theophanies (one
eidetic, the other kinetic), and the dueling wives or sons. Sight and blindness intersect with one of the major deceptions perpetrated upon Jacob,
and barrenness again troubles the patriarch and one of his wives. In addition, Jacob has an impairing encounter with a heavenly figure; he is the
only patriarch to acquire a physical impairment during a theophany. This
cycle contains some interesting variations on the themes, variations that
nevertheless reinforce the narrative prosthetic quality of disability in
Genesis.

A theophany marks Jacob's departure from home. Compared to
Isaac's theophanies, this one has the striking visual motif of the heavenly
stairway (28:12). The divine speech closely parallels those to Abraham
and Isaac, and yet theirs depicted God speaking out of nowhere. Jacob's
first theophany localizes the divine voice in a way that the earlier ones
did not. Only one and a half verses establish this strong visual component, and perhaps only in contrast to this encounter does the low or non-
existent visuality of the other theophanies appear. After this episode, the
narrative resumes Jacob's journey with a geographical orientation (29:1).
Once oriented, the language draws attention to sight:

וירא והנה באר בשדה

He saw: there was a well in the field… (29:2)[38]

A description of the place precedes his dialogue with the shepherds.
These turn out to be Laban's men, and Jacob soon meets Rachel. The
first verb that represents an action of Jacob's toward Rachel is "to see"
(ראה, 29:10a). The men have already told him that this task must be
done, but sight prompts him where words did not. These details may
seem rather humble, perhaps insignificant; what else would he do first?
But the question is not what he would do, but rather what the narrator

38. My translation.

shows him doing, and shows in contrast to the representative elements of other passages. The theophany could be as solely auditory as Isaac's or some of Abraham's, and a Hebrew narrator can get a patriarch to his wife without mentioning vision. Both Abraham and Isaac manage to get married without the benefit of this verb (12:29; 24:67). The visual cues in both the theophany and the well scene contrast with the representation of young Jacob in his auditory parental household, as if the narrator has to re-make him as a visual being when he leaves home and enters a foreign land as a young man. The new prominence of his vision is not necessarily a good thing, much less fool-proof. If Jacob has not been accustomed to using his vision well—the narrative represents an audio-centric character in a home that verisimilitude would lead us to expect also to be audio-centric—then should we expect such an unpracticed figure to use this sense well?

Visual impairment re-appears with the introduction of Leah. Laban takes Jacob in and soon asks what wages he wants (29:15). Between Laban's question and Jacob's reply, the narrator interposes a brief exposition about Laban's daughters, including this:

ועיני לאה רכות ורחל היתה יפת־תאר

Leah had delicate eyes; Rachel was beautiful in appearance. (29:17)[39]

This is the first we readers see of Leah. Apparently, she has a visual impairment at a young age, but is not entirely blind. Indeed, nowhere in the narrative does she have difficulty navigating her daily life, and in that sense, she is not disabled. Yet her weak vision does seem to affect others' actions toward her, and thus the overall narrative arc of Genesis. The language of this passage suggests the emotional valences that soon emerge.

Grammatically, Leah's *eyes* are in parallel construction with *Rachel* herself. Indeed, the first colon represents Leah by metonym, with the weak eyes standing in for the whole woman. If that were not bad enough for Leah, her two eyes receive the semantic parallelism of Rachel's two

---

39. My translation. The meaning of רכות is not clear; delicacy and fragility seem to be the main denotations. Given the other uses of the term, I do not read this as a compliment to Leah. If it is a term for visual impairment, it differs from the one used of Isaac (27:1), and also from the later expression regarding the aged Jacob (48:10). See below, pp. 80–81. Westermann translates as "dull eyes" (*Genesis*, 204). Driver and Speiser both use "tender" (S. R. Driver, *The Book of Genesis, with Introduction and Notes* [London: Methuen, 1904], 270; E. A. Speiser, *Genesis: Introduction, Translation, and Notes* [New York: Doubleday, 1964], 225).

different kinds of "beautiful," with the last aspect of beauty drawing on the strongest visual term. "Form," after all, can be touched, but "appearance" must be seen. In addition to grammar, the placement suggests much. Leah's weak eyes appear precisely here and nowhere else. The paratactic quality of vv. 17–18 indicates causality without overtly stating it. Jacob could love Rachel because he fell in love at first sight, but that would not be a reason for hostility to another wife. Perhaps he does not love Leah because he was tricked into marrying her; but that comes later. The narrative places Jacob's preferential love directly in conjunction with the different physical attributes of the sisters. Conceivably, Laban could have proposed the bargain of both if Jacob wanted one, but he does not. Laban's trickery suggests both that he is concerned about his elder daughter's marriageability to anyone, and also that he does not think that Jacob wants her. Leah's eyes, then, may disable her by lowering her chances for marriage, and with it, children; in short, they could indirectly cause childlessness. Although her impairment has the opposite effect, the threat of this cardinal female disability lurks behind Laban's actions. Finally, impairment or disability once again carries the narrative. Leah's weak eyes are the leading, if not the only, candidate for the men's behavior toward her.

If Jacob does not love Leah because of her eyes, then her visual impairment has further consequences. The marriage scene ironically plays on visual impairment by having Jacob fail to recognize the woman, even as he consummates the union. He does not notice until morning that he did not get the wife he wanted, after seven years' acquaintance with the sisters. The passage (29:21–25) avoids terms denoting sight, and it is, after all, night. Perhaps, too, Jacob continues to rely more on other senses, rather than on vision. In one more week, Jacob marries Rachel. The narrator makes two distinct statements about Jacob's feelings for the women. The first states a differential love: he loves Rachel more than Leah (29:30). The second statement, which is not direct exposition of Jacob but rather representation of God's perception, employs vision as the means of obtaining important information; it also indicates a much worse emotional climate for Leah.

וירא יהוה כי־שנואה לאה ויפתח את־רחמה ורחל עקרה:

And the Lord saw that Leah was hated, and he opened her womb; but Rachel was barren. (29:31)[40]

---

40. My translation, which is very close to both NRSV and JPS. However, these both translate שנואה as "unloved," but the term is much stronger. "Unloved" could

Again, the crucial information comes through sight—here, God's. More-over, this passage contains two key reversals. Instead of the infertility that could occur for an unmarriageable woman, Leah bears prolifically. Also, without divine intervention, one would expect the loved wife to have children and the hated one not to, if the husband's sexual activity reflects his emotional attachments. Thus the narrative directly attributes Leah's fertility to divine action; Rachel's barrenness lacks such a clear attribution, but the passage easily implies it. Jacob will later assert it outright.

Further, without Jacob's favoritism, God would have no motive to compensate a hated wife. The remark about Rachel's barrenness amounts to a red herring, for it echoes the earlier motif of the barren wife who will eventually bear children and draws us into that particular suspense. However, the earlier cycles should have primed the reader to attend to something else too: whose pregnancies God causes, for that way lies the key descent. The answer, in this case, is Leah's, and the names of her four sons contain a tiny narrative and sensory arc. First, she bears Reuben, "See! A son" and then Shimeon, some kind of derivative from שמע; these two names highlight God's sight and hearing, as opposed to her husband's. As in the representation of characters, so in the order of the sons: sight is most prominent. With the third, Levi, Leah hopes for Jacob's attachment to her, and unknowingly produces the priestly patri-arch. Finally, she appears to give up on her husband and simply relates her fourth son's name to the verb "praise" (אודה): Judah. Then, as if she had been aiming for Judah all along, she stops bearing children (29:35).

The cycle has more twists and turns to make, but this much should be clear already: Jacob's inability to see at night (literally) or to pay enough attention (metaphorically, and perhaps from lack of practice) allows his first, unwanted marriage to occur. His inability or refusal to love Leah draws God's attention, so that the narrative represents Leah's pregnan-cies as results of divine agency. Thus, a combination of Jacob's (meta-phorical) blindness and Leah's divinely granted fertility produce the key descendent. Leah's weak eyes may underlie both Jacob's extreme favor-itism and Leah's fertility. Unlike the Abraham and Isaac cycles, no divine communications tell the parents which son is the important one. After a pause during which the wives compete via their maids, Leah bears two more sons and a daughter. That passage contains the clearest statement, from Leah, that love in Jacob's household is a zero-sum game (30:15).

suggest an indifference that lies far below the scope of this term's meaning in virtually all other cases.

Neither the narrator nor the other characters offer a challenge to Leah's understanding of her situation. She buys her way into her husband's embraces, God listens to her (30:17), and she conceives. Her naming statement at the birth of her sixth son revives a hope for spousal love (30:20). The narrative does little to support her hope, unless the immediate shift to Rachel itself suggests that Leah has reached a turning point.

Before turning to Rachel's infertility, we should note that not every child appears with an element of divine causality. The narrator simply notes Leah's daughter Dinah, with no exposition or dialogue about God's role (30:21). This difference among the children of one wife marks the male gender as more important. Less subtly, perhaps, the maids conceive in the usual way, without a divine hand. According to the narrator, Rachel's maid Bilhah conceives after sexual relations with Jacob. Although Rachel construes this son as divine vindication (30:6), her interpretation is not otherwise narratively supported as Leah's naming statements were. When Rachel names Bilhah's second son, she does not mention God at all but rather refers to the competition with her sister (30:8). That competition continues through Leah's maid Zilpah, whose conceptions occur without narrative credit to God, and whose names do not mention God but instead refer to the ongoing baby race. If we compare the maids only to Rachel, we might infer that God only gets involved when barrenness must be cured or overcome. However, if we compare them to Leah, we find that the narrative distinguishes ordinary from divinely implicated conceptions. Thus we have three categories: divinely implicated fertility, ordinary fertility, and divinely implicated barrenness.[41] The last category encompasses both the period of barrenness and any overcoming of it that will occur. Incidentally, this division of offspring also creates a binary marking of women, for Jacob's two proper wives get the divine attention, while his two concubines do not.

Now, let us remember Rachel. The narrator notes her barrenness before anyone has borne any children, in the ambiguous line discussed above (29:31). A little later, after Leah's first four sons, we find out what the characters themselves make of it. Whereas Leah views her sons as a way to win her husband's love, Rachel construes her sister's prolific reproduction as an affront to herself. She threatens Jacob with her own death by unstated means (30:1). Suicide is a possible implication, although the language does not indicate a self-reflexive action. At any

---

41. The general Near Eastern view would implicate God or the gods in all fertility or lack thereof. Against the backdrop of that common belief, this narrative makes further distinctions.

rate, the threat angers Jacob, who refuses responsibility and blames God for her barrenness (30:2). His interpretation accords with the common beliefs of the time and place. The narrator may or may not agree; the ambiguity may be deliberate. If this narrator can represent fertility as ordinary or extraordinary, then he could make a similar distinction about infertility. This possible distinction implies somewhat different modes of divine intervention later: if God has caused Rachel's barrenness, then her fertility reverses a divine policy; but if the infertility occurs naturally, then God corrects a state of affairs for which God was not responsible. The narrator is just suggestive enough to pose the problem, and coy enough not to resolve it.

In any case, when Rachel enters the rank of mothers, the narrator and the characters both ascribe credit to God, in addition to noting the social disrespect that accompanied infertility (30:22–24a). For the first time, Rachel's ascription of divine involvement has support in the narrator's representation of the deity. The passage surely has its place in the barrenness-overcome motif, but comparison to the other cases shows an important difference. When Sarah conceives, the narrator iterates that the conception complies with an earlier promise to or about Sarah (Gen 21:1–2). Unlike Sarah, Rebekah does not receive a specific promise prior to her pregnancy, but she inquires and receives an oracle before the twins are born (25:23). In Rachel's case, no promises have been given, no prophecies made. Nor does Rachel seem to have any expectations beyond the naming-wish for another one of these (30:23–24). Joseph will be important, as the redactor's audience surely knew, but he is not marked in the same way as Isaac and Jacob were. Indeed, God and Jacob seem to have rather different views about which wife matters most.

After Rachel's fertility and Joseph's birth, the childbearing competition pauses for Jacob's return home. Laban threatens his departure, and Esau his return. In his conflict with Laban, Rachel's theft of the idols brings the greatest danger, at least to her life, and perhaps to the whole group. She conceals the theft with a ruse: she pleads temporary immobility on account of her period, as she sits on hidden contraband. Jacob and Laban mark their parting agreement with a stone pillar and dialogue that highlights visual contact and God's watchfulness in its absence (31:46–50).[42] The concern with God's ability to see without regard to distance seems ironic between two men who have both tricked each other when

---

42. Jacob's double reference to God as "the dread of Isaac" employs a term with primarily kinesthetic and secondarily auditory associations. See Gen 31:44, 53. Other divine names or epithets are not particularly visual, but the association of this term with Isaac pointedly foregrounds non-visual sensory modes.

they were in mutual sight. Although the narrator foregrounds the property dispute and its settlement, the visual terms provide a reprise of those in Jacob's arrival—once more, with irony.

Jacob's encounter with Esau is also fraught, and the narrator builds up suspense by keeping to Jacob's limited point of view. The messengers disclose Esau's party of four hundred men, but Jacob does not know his intentions. He sends the gifts of cattle ahead, crosses the Jabbok, and encamps for the night. Like the flight theophany, this one highlights a visual element in a way that the Abrahamic and Isaacic theophanies do not (32:31–32). The encounter also gives Jacob a mobility impairment—a limp. In his discussion of this passage, Wynn engages two important questions about this episode. First, Wynn critiques Brueggemann, Rosenblatt, and others for viewing Jacob as a tragic hero on account of the crippling.[43] Nothing in the text, he notes, supports a tragic-cripple view of Jacob. On the contrary, Jacob can maintain his grip and win the wrestling match even after sustaining the injury. The angel's re-naming speech concedes that Jacob has "prevailed" (32:29).[44] Second, there is the question whether the impairment is permanent. No textual evidence indicates that his limp that morning went away later. In the absence of such evidence, Wynn contends: "Any attempt to make the disability temporary is an attempt to deny Jacob's disability and to reestablish his normate status."[45]

In fact, Wynn regards the impaired limb as Jacob's sign of the covenant.[46] I would supplement Wynn's interpretation with the observation that the later narrative does not indicate that Jacob's limp hinders his functioning in any important way. Jacob's limp may be an anomaly in a narrative so concerned with male vision and female infertility; nevertheless, at a pivotal, initiatory moment, God delivers a disability to his patriarch. Jacob will lose his vision, too, or so it seems.

A full analysis of the Joseph Cycle, with Judah's prominent role, lies beyond the scope of this study. Alter discussed the significance of recognition as a motif that links Jacob, Judah, and Joseph.[47] I would add that these recognitions and their failures—of Joseph's cloak, of Judah's pledges, of one's relatives—all depend on visual cues, and thus continue

43. Wynn, "Normate Hermeneutic," 96–98.
44. Wynn (ibid., 98) quarrels with Westermann's demon hypothesis and von Rad's attempts to isolate sources because he thinks that the injured man cannot go on to win. I concur with his critiques.
45. Ibid., 99.
46. Ibid., 100
47. Robert Alter, *Art of Biblical Narrative* (New York: Basic, 1981), 4–11.

the narrative's variations on themes of vision and its significance or lack thereof. The Joseph Cycle would thus be a good site for a sensory-critical study; it relates to disability motifs only as both occur within a narrative that is interested in vision and fertility. Thus I shall omit this portion of Genesis, and close with the old Jacob's problematic visual capacity.

A brief comparison of the descriptions of each character's vision reveals some subtle shading of each case; not everyone is blind in the same way. The terms for visual impairment differ from those used of Isaac and Leah. Isaac's eyes grow dim (ותכהין), a term that includes the idea of faintness. Its denotations suggest movement from one state to another, as does the imperfect form of the verb. Even apart from the representational analysis above, the descriptive language in that one verse suggests a progressive condition. The description of Leah's visual condition omits a verb, using a gapped predicate adjective. As noted above, the term רכות connotes delicacy and fragility rather than decline from a prior state. Finally, the narrator describes Jacob's vision in advanced age thus:

ועיני ישראל כבדו מזקן לא יוכל לראות

Israel's eyes were dull from age; he was not able to see. (Gen 48:10)[48]

כבד is used elsewhere of sensory impairment, but its use for Jacob, in particular, suggests that vision has been a burden to him, one he cannot carry any longer. As with his father, the word choice for his blindness fits with the earlier representation of his visuality. Jacob did not always use his eyes well or easily. In a way, he is the mirror image of his father: if Isaac prospered without using vision much or at all, Jacob seems to have done as well as he has not because of his eyes, but in spite of them.

The notice of his blindness, however, occurs in a context in which he sees quite a lot, and I do not mean "see" metaphorically. At his final visit with Joseph, Jacob sees his two grandsons (48:8). He then remarks about getting to see both Joseph and the grandsons (48:11), with forms of ראה used twice. The verse noting that he cannot see is thus framed by his seeing, represented in exposition and dialogue. This kind of disjunction can be read as an indication of different sources, but that would not answer the representational question. Can Jacob see, or not? And does this matter? The ensuing narrative does not resolve the first question, for it shows him crossing his hands to bless the grandsons and resisting Joseph's correction. Sighted or not, he knows what he intends. The reversed blessing, of course, alludes to Isaac's blessing of his sons, only

48. My translation.

Jacob clearly acts in full knowledge. In both cases, the patriarch's blindness serves as cover for contravening the expected primogeniture; it also marks as special the action of preference for the younger. As for whether vision matters, that seems to depend on who one is and on what the narrator wants to say about election and God.

The double motifs of patriarchal blindness and matriarchal infertility thus use disability for certain narrative purposes. Among patriarchal couples, at least one partner is disabled most of the (narrative) time. The preferred son is marked by the disability of at least one parent, a disability that plays a key role in establishing that son's status. Sarah's barrenness requires divine activity and marks Isaac; Isaac's blindness enables the fulfillment of Rebekah's oracle and marks Jacob. With Jacob, the motif bifurcates. Along one line, Jacob's failure to use his vision marries him to Leah of the fragile eyes, and his refusal to love her endears her to God, such that her fertility gains divine attention and marks Judah. Along another line, Rachel's infertility eventually catches the divine attention and thus marks Joseph. In the long-term economy of preference, however, Joseph's function is to protect the others, especially Judah (45:5–8; 50:18–21). Jacob's blessing in Gen 49, although an ancient and independent poem, fits well with these motifs. It maintains the apparently dual election of Judah and Joseph, while representing Joseph as a defender and singling out Judah for an *ex post facto* prophecy of monarchy. Whatever disparate sources may be combined, each of the key figures is marked by disability in parent, spouse, or self. Beyond the static notion of marking, the patriarchal cycles conform to Mitchell's and Snyder's concept of narrative prosthesis. Without disability—infertility overcome, deeply ambiguous blindnesses, or interesting limps—Genesis would be almost entirely episodic. Finally, a major theological point depends on this narrative prosthesis, for the characters' disabilities give God something to do to demonstrate power and to make his selections among humans. In short, the disabled characters actually prop up the representation of God's power and providence.

## Job and Aesthetic Transcendence

In his "Preface to the Hebrew Bible," literary critic George Steiner suggests that the book of Job does not answer the questions it poses, but rather draws the reader through a certain experience: "At every reading, the vehement depths, the unanswerabilities in this text, open again into a kind of raging light."[49] I take Steiner's remarks as a starting point for two

49.  Steiner, "A Preface to the Hebrew Bible," 72.

exegetical problems, one old, one new. The old problem is that the divine speeches do not directly engage the dialogue that precedes them. Are they connected to the other speeches at all, and if so, how? Can an aesthetic response answer a moral challenge? The new exegetical problem is reading the book of Job in light of contemporary disability studies, for each can enhance our understanding of the other. These two problems turn out to be intimately related; that is, a reading that privileges Job's articulation of his disabled body can shed "a kind of raging light" on God's speeches.

## Job as Disabled
Why should Job be viewed as disabled, rather than as someone suffering from a disease, and a temporary one at that? The ancient author would not have thought of his protagonist in those terms. On the contrary, the meaning of the contemporary term "disabled" fits Job with little or no distortion, for the author depicts Job in terms that significantly overlap with the main components of the concept. Job's affliction, at its primary and simplest level, is an unnamed skin disease. Since the effects of the disease significantly impair his daily life, he is also disabled. His own self-descriptions comport with this analysis: in 30:16–19, he details his disabled and diseased body, and contrasts his current situation with his former, able-bodied life (29:15–16). Indeed, he cannot—is not able to— do anything else except scrape his sores and lament. He is confined to his ash-heap, as it were. Beyond these physical aspects of his condition, there is the protagonist's vivid and deeply felt sense of a rift between his body and his social world (ch. 19 in its entirety, and 30:9–15). I will analyze this feature of the book in more detail below. These two factors of physical limitation and social-emotional isolation from the able-bodied comport well with historical and contemporary reports of disability.

   This justification for applying a contemporary concept to an ancient text lies within the realm of hermeneutics. However, the history of interpretation provides a second and rather different rationale for this project. For centuries, Job has been the paradigmatic sufferer. To the extent that the book has been used to tell people how to experience a disease or disability (a social pressure one can see at work in the text itself), the history of this use falls under the purview of the history of disability. Take, for instance, the proverbial "patience of Job."[50] We

---

50. Marvin Pope noted a generation ago that whatever else Job might be, he is not patient. But the proverb's hold on the popular imagination remains strong, if I may judge from the essays of my Bible-saturated students. Marvin Pope, *Job: A New Translation with Introduction and Commentary* (New York: Doubleday, 1965), xv.

cannot know if the author of the letter of James was talking about our book of Job, or some other, more pious version of the folk-tale when he used "the patience of Job" (5:11) as a model.[51] But we do know that biblical interpreters took their key to the book of Job from the phrase in James. The authority of the proverb, together with the same rage for order that drives Job's friends, engenders misreading. Literary critic Harold Bloom uses this term for misunderstandings so powerful that they compete with and often obscure the text itself. If the proverbial expression is an interpretation of the book of Job, it is clearly a misreading. A weak or strong one? It is weak in its failure to perceive much in the text, to insist on the simplicities that obtain before one arrives at Job's situation. Yet this failure also betrays a kind of strength, the strength of resistance to Job's own account of himself and his suffering, that is to say, the power of refusal enjoyed by Job's able-bodied, healthy friends. This power is contagious: readers catch it from the friends, and perjure themselves in defense of God. I do not mean to take on and refute a proverb and the misreadings it has engendered. Instead, I propose to turn the tables. Rather than focusing on theodicy (the able-bodied friends' project), let us attend to Job's language of physical suffering, dismemberment, and monstrosity. Careful attention to these images provides insight into the divine speeches and, through them, to the book as a whole.

*Basic Approaches to the Book of Job*
Interpretations of the book of Job generally fall into two categories, with a few exceptions. Of the two major types, one is the pious, find-fault-with-Job-to-vindicate-God approach, and the other is the impious, defiant, God-is-a-sadist interpretation.[52] Both proposals accept a theodicy construction of the text that leaves readers with an either/or choice: either God is right, or Job is. Certainly the friends advocate this construction and the first answer to it. However, the friends' views are so thoroughly undermined by Job, by God's speeches, and then by the ending, that

51. Roland Murphy (*The Tree of Life: An Exploration of Biblical Wisdom Literature* [3d. ed.; Grand Rapids: Eerdmans, 2002], 33–48) notes that this KJV translation of *hypomene* is inaccurate. Nevertheless, the English phrase does serve as a lens through which Job is seen by readers of that translation.

52. Normal Habel gives four types: (1) Job surrenders completely, (2) Job reconciles with God, (3) Job placates God with an ironic capitulation, or (4) Job spurns God as an unjust power. This quartet can be further reduced to two if we realize that the first pair represent a rapprochement and differ only in degree, whereas the second pair represent a breach, and differ also in degree (*The Book of Job: A Commentary* [Philadelphia: Westminster, 1985], 577–78).

readers should question this construction itself.[53] Rather, we should follow the text in questioning, on a fundamental level, this binary opposition. I shall briefly review the limitations of both sides of theodicy's either/or structure.

Interpretations that find fault with Job, either before or after his suffering begins, deserve consideration at the outset because they deny something that I take to be axiomatic: Job's innocence. God affirms it at the beginning and end (1:8; 2:3; 42:7–8), thus indicating that neither a prior sin nor one committed in the course of the dialogues can explain Job's suffering. Further, the divine speeches do not indict Job of wrongdoing, when this is exactly what Job has asked for (13:23). This is not to say that Job is presented as a perfect being, but only that the undeserved nature of his suffering is undeniable. To explain the suffering by finding fault with Job is to cling to the tidy worldview that the book seems bent on demolishing. In addition to these difficulties, this approach fails to account for what God does and does not say in the divine speeches. If this interpretation were correct, one would expect an explanation of why suffering is really good for you, along the lines proposed by Elihu (33:16–17).[54] But no divine rationale for Job's suffering is given. Further,

53. There are interpretations that do not fit this typology. Atypical proposals include Robert Gordis's mild aesthetic interpretation in *The Book of God and Man: A Study of Job* (Chicago: University of Chicago Press, 1965), and *The Book of Job: Commentary, New Translation, and Special Studies* (New York: Jewish Theological Seminary of America, 1978); J. Gerald Janzen's creation theology account in his commentary *Job* (Atlanta: John Knox, 1985); Edwin M. Good's polysemous and ironic reading in *In Turns of Tempest: A Reading of Job with a Translation* (Stanford: Stanford University Press, 1990); David Wolfers's reading of Job as an allegory of the exile (*Deep Things Out of Darkness: The Book of Job, Essays and a New English Translation* [Grand Rapids: Eerdmans, 1995]); and Carol A. Newsom's recent work *The Book of Job: A Contest of Moral Imaginations* (Oxford: Oxford University Press, 2003). I will discuss several of these in more detail below.

54. I agree with the consensus that these chapters are probably an insertion, and yet I favor reading the text we have instead of one we do not. Pope summarizes the consensus that the Elihu speeches are additions (*Job*, xxvii–xxviii). Habel disagrees and proposes a reading that makes these speeches integral to the text. The possibility of interpreting the text we have does not, however, refute the arguments in favor of treating these speeches as additions. Murphy, referencing D. N. Freedman, notes that Elihu provides a literary transition but can also be seen as a reader trying to add to the discussion (*Tree of Life*, 42). Newsom fully develops this insight in her chapter "The Dissatisfied Reader: Elihu and the Historicity of the Moral Imagination," in *Book of Job*, 200–33. Given her use of the Bakhtinian dialogic structure, the compositional history of the text takes second place to a polyphonic structure that includes many voices without resolving them.

this line of interpretation reduces the speeches to assertions of divine power. To be sure, there are passages about God's omnipotence and Job's ignorance in the speeches. However, if this is all the speeches say or do, God is left insisting only that God can do whatever God wants. Nobody was arguing that. Finally, this reading fails to account for most of the content of the divine speeches. Surely anything would do to demonstrate divine power, so why carry on about cosmic forces, wild animals, and most bizarre of all, Leviathan and Behemoth? It is possible that the selection has no rationale, but an interpretation that can account for the content would have greater explanatory value than one that does not.

The second type of reading with which I disagree can be characterized as the impious, defiant, God-is-a-sadist interpretation.[55] It has the virtue of accounting for just about everything in the book, and I find it far more cogent than the pious interpretation. However, since my disagreement with it is subtle and tentative, I postpone discussion of it until I have demonstrated what a disabled reading can do. At this point, it will suffice to note that this interpretation also fails to account for the content of the divine speeches. Like the pious interpretation, it takes the speeches as sheer assertions of power, and thus as lengthy repetitions of something that was never at issue. While an author might understand and depict God in that way, I do not think that the author of Job is doing this. The ironies are too clear, the poetry too sublime, and the demolition of the friends' either/or thinking too thorough for the book to be an endorsement of the other side of this simplistic scheme.[56] The sadistic interpretation accounts for something in Job's (and our) experience, at the expense of accounting for the book.

Finally, some interpreters try to split the difference between Job and God. Habel, for instance, uses literary analysis to argue for the integrity of both the book and Job. On a formal level, he unifies much. However, at the key moment of the theophany, Habel backs away from any positive proposal that would take us beyond the either/or scheme. He finds fault with Job: Job did not know everything, and God offers these

55.   As exemplified by John Briggs Curtis, "On Job's Response to Yahweh," *JBL* 98 (1979): 497–511. Mark Twain took a similarly dim view of theodicies, but he was not a biblical scholar.

56.   Rachel Magdalene has recently made the case that Near Eastern prayer forms employing legal formulae underlie the structure of Job and several of his key speeches. Although I find the parallels convincing, I do not think that they alone indicate what the author is doing with them. Rachel Magdalene, "The Ancient Near Eastern Origins of Impairment as Theological Disability and the Book of Job," *Perspectives in Religious Studies*, 34, no. 1 (2007): 23–60.

mysteries in order to bring Job to this insight.[57] Murphy, too, acknowledges Job's innocent suffering, and says that the book leaves us with
a mystery beyond human understanding.[58] Janzen places the divine
speeches in the context of Israel's creation theology and the human role
of stewardship within the cosmic order.[59] His comparisons to other
portions of the biblical corpus are interesting, and the allusions are
probably deliberate on the poet's part. However, Janzen's analysis takes
the speeches very far afield from the book of Job itself, with the result
that God's speeches editorialize about something that might be true, but
the reader is left wondering why these things are being said in this
context. Habel, Murphy, and Janzen all make overtures to an aesthetic
element in the speeches, but they tend to resort to "mystery" rather than
pushing the aesthetic idea all the way. Good, Gordis, and Newsom do
argue for a serious aesthetic case to these speeches, and their views will
be engaged in more detail below. The trouble with terms such as mystery, contradiction, or polyphonic voices is that they neither get God off
the moral hook nor venture into what would happen if something other
than morality structures the cosmos. What does the rehearsal of mysterious things *accomplish*?

*Job and the Monsters*
In order to understand how the monsters function in the divine speeches,
we must first examine some references to them in the dialogue. Job and
the friends make several allusions to primordial monsters. Further, these
allusions are connected to other motifs. Two motifs in particular provide
the foundations for my reading of the divine speeches: Job and the
monsters as objects of divine attack, and the connection between attention and suffering.[60] These motifs emerge in the dialogue, with subtle
connections between them. The divine speeches then bring monstrosity
and attention together into an experience that resembles aesthetic arrest
and the perception of the sublime, but differs crucially from both by
including the perceiver (Job) as part of the perception (the monstrous
magnificent).

　　Allusions to the primordial monsters occur near the beginning and end
of Job's dialogue with the friends. Between their appearances, the

　57.　Habel, *Job*, 536.
　58.　Murphy, *Tree of Life*, 46.
　59.　Janzen, *Job*, 233–47.
　60.　This is not to ignore the law-suit metaphors in the dialogue. The legal language provides structure and the plot impetus by which God responds to Job's sub-
poena. It does not, however, elucidate much of the content of the divine speeches.

speeches in which Job details his own physical dismemberment occur. To be sure, there is much between the monsters' brief appearances and their curtain call, but the language of divine attack links them to Job's descriptions of his body and experience. I will treat the monsters first, and then examine their relevance to a suffering human body.

Job's state is described at the end of the frame story's introduction (2:7–8), but Job says little directly about his physical suffering. His first speech, in ch. 3, casts his day of birth outside of time. The language returns Job's beginning to before the world's beginning, thus undoing it. Among the cosmic figures of light and darkness, birth and death, v. 8 contains at least one, and perhaps two, references to primordial monsters:

יקבהו אררי־יום
העתידים ירר לויתן

Let the Sea-cursers damn it,
Those skilled to stir Leviathan[61]

The reading of "Leviathan" is uncontested, and marks the first appearance of this figure. Further, Pope and others emend Yam, on the basis of the parallel use of Yam with Leviathan and similar figures in other locations (Ps 74:13–14; Job 7:12; Isa 27:1).[62] Whether we have here one primordial monster or two, the parallels in Babylonian and Ugaritic myths have long been noted. Their mention characterizes the chaotic world before creation, to which Job consigns his day of birth. Further, the monsters are subjected to an ordering power, the agents of which remain vague in this verse. Job wishes that these agents would do to his day of birth what they did to Leviathan and Yam. What Job implies in ch. 3 is spelled out directly in 7:12:

הים־אני אם־תנין
כי־תשים עלי משמר

Am I the Sea or the Dragon,
That you set a guard over me?

This verse draws a comparison between Job and the primordial monsters: God's action toward Job resembles God's action toward the monsters, to wit, attack and dismemberment. Janzen noted that the term משמר echoes the terms used for siege attack against chaos monsters in Near Eastern epic.[63] Further, since the grammatical form is a rhetorical question with a

61. In this section, translations are Pope's (*Job*), unless noted otherwise.
62. Ibid., 30.
63. On משמר, see J. G. Janzen, "Another Look at God's Watch Over Job (7:12)," *JBL* 108 (1989): 109–16.

clearly implied No,[64] Job is *not* comparing his importance or strength to that of the monsters.[65] The effect is rather the opposite: "Could I be as threatening as a monster, that God would attack me in the same way? Of course not." The passage thus indicates some mode of identification with monsters, together with a differentiation from them. Job suggests that all the really big chaos monsters were taken care of before creation, and if he were such a thing, he too should not exist within creation; but he is not such a thing, so the attack does not make sense.

The monsters' reappearance in ch. 26 is framed by contrasting characterizations of the friends' speech and Job's own. To Bildad, Job replies that his speech lacks power (26:2–4). The term for breath, נשמה, is used of both human and divine breath in the book of Job and elsewhere in the Bible. Here, Job implies that Bildad's (and the friends') breath is powerless because it is unauthorized. By contrast, Job's breath is authorized and his words thus powerful: his nostrils have God's breath (27:3–4), and that guarantees the truth and power of his utterances.

These two references to breath and to the power of speech frame the monsters' most elaborate appearance in the discourses:

בכחו רגע הים...
ברוחו שמים שפרה...
הן־אלה קצות דרכו
ומה־שמץ דבר נשמע־בו
ורעם גבורתו מי יתבונן

By his power he quelled the Sea...
By his wind, he bagged the Sea...
Lo, these are but bits of his power;
What a faint whisper we hear of him!
Who could attend his mighty roar? (26:12–14)[66]

64. On the rhetorical question structure, see David Diewert, "Job 7:12," *JBL* 106 (1987): 203–15.

65. Timothy K. Beal, in his *Religion and Its Monsters* (New York: Routledge, 2002), portrays Job as aligning himself with the monsters and against God, in order to curse all creation and return everything to primordial chaos (pp. 35–43). Delightful as this book is, Beal goes too far: Job's curses are highly directed at his day of birth, that is, at his own experience as the locus of chaos that should have been undone before creation.

66. Pope assigns most of ch. 26 to Bildad's third speech, and regards the whole as mythical. I do not find this re-arrangement necessary. Although Bildad's third speech is unusually short, ch. 25 harps on the friends' ongoing theme of human guilt before God, a theme that is missing from the mythical material of ch. 26, but very much present in Job's own allusions and in the divine address to Job alone.

Taken together, these passages set up an antithetical pair of associations: mere breath (נשמה) yields powerless words (לא־בח), but real breath (רוח) accomplishes real things (דבר). The former pair characterizes the friends' speech. The latter pair characterizes both Job and God, with a difference: while both God and Job are said to possess רוח God performs things by means of it, and Job simply speaks correctly about those things.

Another analogy lies within this structure. Job accuses the friends of attempting to subdue him as God subdued the monsters, but they literally lack the breath to accomplish the task. He will not be out-argued. But the passage also contrasts God's power over the monsters with the friends' impotence over Job (26:2–4). Their words may wound him, but will not bring him down fatally. This comparison further implies that it is the friends, and not Job, who speak arrogantly, a charge he made earlier in legal terms (13:7–10). In another sense, he re-states his similarity to the forces of chaos, which he seems to have inferred from the divine attack itself. The context adds a twist to Job's earlier qualified identification with the monsters. In both his suffering and his speech, Job places himself inside the realm of divine attack and divine sustenance, but he places the friends outside. In both cases, Job likens himself to the monsters: only a divine reply will silence him. Again, I do not intend to suggest that Job considers himself equal *in power* to the monsters; the similarity lies in being the *objects of divine attack*. Only in contrast to the friends is Job (are his words) as powerful as monsters. There may also be a shift in Job's placement of the monsters. In this passage, they seem to be marginal parts of creation that testify to God's power and, in a way, to their own, as figures who can absorb the divine attack, even though it defeats them. The shift indicates ambivalence about the role of monsters in creation—a rather subtle point to which the divine speeches profusely respond.

These references to the monsters occur near the beginning and end of the discourses. In the middle speeches, Job articulates more specifically his experience as a disabled, even dismembered, human body. The language and causes of dismemberment are one of the bones of contention between Job and the friends. The images of dismemberment go beyond the skin disease described in 2:7–8. In 16:8–17, Job gives a long description of himself. He begins with "shriveled" and "gaunt," both descriptions of skin disease, and proceeds quickly to a full dismemberment of the body (16:12–16).[67] The description escalates from wounds to an

67. J. G. Janzen has compared, in detail, the siege vocabulary of ch. 16 to Marduk's stratagems against Tiamat in *Enuma Elish* ("Another Look," *JBL* 108 [1989]:

occlusion of vision. After a short protest to God for his own suffering and the friends' lack of understanding, Job reverses the sequence, going from blindness to disintegration:

> My eye is dimmed with anguish,
> My limbs are all like a shadow...
> But the righteous retains his force,
> The clean-handed grows in strength...
> My days are done,
> My plans shattered,
> My heart's desires. (17:7–11)

With the rhetorical chiasmus complete, Job concludes in Sheol (17:13–16). He verbally co-operates with his own dismemberment by articulating what God has done.

At this point in the dialogue, Job has complained several times about the friends' lack of understanding (6:14–21; 12:2–4; 13:4–5; 16:2–5). Now Bildad objects that Job is the agent of his own dismemberment (18:4). This charge allows Job extend the physical images to his social and psychological isolation: not only is he torn apart physically, but he is torn from the community of other human beings (19:13–20). Beyond the social effects of his physical condition, the friends' words are also attacks that further dismember him (19:2). In sum, the mythological images of divine attack on monsters converge with Job's description of physical dismemberment. In all likelihood, the allusions were intentional. As we shall see, the descriptions of Behemoth and Leviathan draw from the same pool of images.

*Divine Attention*
Since the divine speeches do not directly engage the topics of the dialogue, they raise the question what Job, or a reader, is supposed to attend to. In order to answer this, we must consider the role of attention in the dialogue. Both Job and the friends draw connections between suffering and attention (or inattention), and both discuss the proper direction of one's attention. By "attention," I mean a state indicated by a certain cluster of Hebrew terms: (1) the verbs בכן and שׁית, with the object לבב, which express internal attention; (2) the verb שׁמר with a direct object, or שׁית, with the object לבב or לב and an indirect object, which express attention directed externally; and (3) terms of remembering and forgetting, for example, שׁכח, זכר, and synonyms. The book of Job represents attention as an activity of both human and divine figures.

109–16). This is one of the passages for which he notes parallels in Babylonian myth.

Job agrees with conventional wisdom in that he claims that divine attention causes human suffering. But the attention, and thus the suffering, lack all proportion. Newsom notes that prayer—the usual means of directing both human and divine attention—is "disarticulated" by Job.[68] Her discussion focuses on the human paranoia and divine sadism implicit in too much attention; here, I am simply laying part of the foundation for my interpretation of the divine speeches. Job depicts a hyper-attentive God who is eerily present in awareness but absent in speech. Thus Job portrays himself as a victim of divine *attention*, not divine inattention (10:12–14a). Even sleep cannot provide an escape from the horror of divine regard (7:14–15). Job extends this experience to humankind in general when he asks why God bothers paying any attention to human beings at all (7:17–18). He then suggests that a little less divine attention would make for a more pleasant life—or, failing that, enough time to swallow (7:19): "Will you never look away from me? / Leave me be till I swallow my spittle?" For Job, God's attention is part of God's attack on him.

Yet it is not attention alone that brings his suffering to such a pitch, but rather the combination of divine presence and absence. God is painfully near, but imperceptible (9:11 12). One feels the divine presence in suffering, but God does not remain to answer questions (9:15–16). Without a dialogue partner, Job's attention becomes fixed upon himself—a fixation that he wants to overcome, but cannot (9:27–28). Since self-forgetfulness, either in life or in death, is beyond him, the only possible action is speech (7:11; 10:1; 13:3; 19:8–9; 21:3–6). Failing that, he addresses God and wonders why, if God was paying so much attention to him that he suffers from it, God will not attend enough to enter into dialogue with him. This is not to suggest that Job wants an explanation; would any explanation, much less the one to which the reader is privy, suffice? Job describes a rather different sort of torture, a consciousness of God's attention coupled with a refusal of God's communication. So Job gives up on dialogue, even in the form of a trial, and asks for oblivion (e.g. 6:8–9; 7:14–16; 10:20–21).

Typically, the friends miss Job's point. Bildad, who responds to the second speech, argues that forgetfulness of God causes suffering (8:13). To insist on human inattentiveness as the cause of suffering overlooks Job's scrupulous attention to God both before and during his ordeal. Further, the reply is not to Job's point. Bildad is offering a remedy for suffering, but the remedy ignores the cause of suffering and thus says nothing about Job's claim that too much divine attention is not a good

68. Newsom, *Job*, 136–38.

thing. In the next cycle, it falls to Zophar to recommend that Job turn his mind to God, and if he were to do so, "Then could you lift up a face unblemished; / You might be steadfast and undaunted" (11:13–15). To say this, Zophar ignores Job's pleas that God tell him exactly what is wrong with him. Job has never claimed that God was not watching him or does not know anything about him. However, he does say that God ignores the wicked (21:14–15). Eliphaz, in a direct reply to this passage, claims that the wicked do get what is coming to them. But in order to make this argument, he attributes to Job the view that God does not know everything (22:12–14). Like Zophar and Bildad, Eliphaz misses the point. Job did not say that God's knowledge was imperfect. Job specifically rejects this assumption in his final speech (31:4). This premise may be the only one that would lead *Eliphaz* to conclude that the wicked prosper. But *Job* starts with observation of his own life, not with a theological premise. One might say that their different views about divine attention arise from the different starting points for their own attention: Job attends first of all to his experience of suffering and of God, and the friends attend to their theological premise, which they want to vindicate at the cost of denying Job's experience. Because of the mismatch, the friends constantly fail to perceive the basis of Job's claims.

## The Divine Speeches

Before the divine speeches begin, the dialogue has set up certain associations in an unstable structure. Job compares the divine attack on himself to the divine attack on the chaos monsters of myth. None of the interlocutors disagree with this comparison; the trouble is how to place it in a cosmic structure. Job is both like and unlike these monsters. Just as the monsters exist on the margins, before creation or in the still-chaotic sea, so also the chaotic (crippled) human body is ostracized to the margins of the social world (19:13–20). His defeated body and isolation from human society make him a monster of sorts, on a small scale. The friends reason that if God is attacking Job, Job must indeed have slipped into sin (chaos). In this view, God is the righteous agent of order, and Job is a small-time chaos monster. On the other hand, Job has lived his life to the highest standards of ethical conduct (emphasized in the dialogue) and ritual observance (emphasized in the prologue). His final statement of his innocence (chs. 29–31) reasserts the ethical structure; if Job is not really a monster, his treatment as one is wrong. In either case, someone, either Job or God, is acting chaotically and must be a monster. The two major types of interpretation differ over the choice of monster. If the divine speeches are read merely as assertions of God's power, then these mutually exclusive structures are left intact, and one chooses between them, finding fault with Job or with God.

However, the divine speeches change the terms. They undermine some of the fundamental assumptions of both structures by re-aligning key comparisons. First of all, the Near Eastern myths that underlie the references to Yam, Tehom, the Serpent, and so on, all depict these monsters as forces that are defeated before creation, as a precondition to it. Even in the discourse of Job and his friends, they lurk on the margins, held at bay by God but not really part of the ordered cosmos. God's second speech (chs. 40–41) is nothing short of a hymn to Behemoth and Leviathan.[69] They are held forth as marvels of God's creative power. To be sure, they remain outside of human society. In that sense, they are the two most wonderful creatures in a menagerie of odd things that exist beyond the human social world.[70] Rather than agents of chaos who were defeated, dismembered, and disbarred from cosmic order, God describes the monstrous as magnificent. Cosmic order is thus re-calibrated without the human center assumed by Job and his friends. From this new perspective, the monsters are central and human conduct is marginal. Thus the speeches reverse the most fundamental assumption that the discourse made about the monstrous.

The divine speeches also re-align the comparisons and contrasts that Job set up. He compared the divine attack against him to the divine attack against primordial enemies. But if these enemies are not really

69. A few decades ago, the consensus favored the view that Behemoth was the hippopotamus and Leviathan the crocodile. For a thorough discussion of the weaknesses in this position, see Good, *Tempest*, 358–62, and for the mythic background, see Pope, *Job*, 320–32. Even advocates of the hippo–croc hypothesis concede that the imagery does not entirely fit. I hold with the mythic interpretation for the following reasons: the poet can describe animals with an accuracy that does not open the descriptions to dispute; these descriptions do not fit well; hippos and crocodiles can be fought and captured, and (contra Gordis, *Job*, 558) the products of the latter can be used by humans; and the parallels to Near Eastern myths are pervasive. This is not to deny any correspondence between observable beasts and these two. In my opinion, Behemoth and Leviathan are textbook illustrations of David Hume's thesis that our ideas of things we do not experience are composites based on things we do experience.

70. Avalos argues that the book of Job is visiocentric because of its copious visuality, through which much important information is transmitted (*TAB*, 55–58). In response, Bruce Birch objects that Avalos overstates the case and ignores important auditory features in Job ("Impairment as a Condition in Biblical Scholarship," in *TAB*, 185–95 [see p. 193 for the criticism of Avalos]). I myself regard Job as extremely vivid in several modes, and not decisively favoring one.

opponents in a pre-creation cosmic combat, but rather artifacts in the portfolio of divine wonders, then the ground has been pulled out from under the initial comparison. Newsom has argued recently that Behemoth resembles Job, and Leviathan resembles God:

> As placid strength was the hallmark of Behemoth, so fearsome violence is the characteristic of Leviathan…there is a curious level of identification between God and Leviathan. God represents himself as being in the image of Leviathan, only more so. Indeed, as has often been pointed out, the physical description of Leviathan is uncannily evocative of the theophanic descriptions of God.[71]

I do not see a clear one-on-one analogy of Behemoth to Job and Leviathan to God; perhaps Newsom's claim is not intended to be so tidy. In any case, the proposed similarity between the monsters and Job, on the one hand, and God, on the other, requires elaboration.

There are striking verbal parallels between Behemoth and Job, but the same set of terms are used in very different ways in reference to each figure. Behemoth is introduced by reference to his power:

הנה־נא כחו במתניו
ואנו בשרירי בטנו

    See the strength in his loins,
    The power in his massive belly. (40:16)

The word כח, "power, strength, ability," is a loaded term in the book of Job. Job uses it frequently for what he no longer has (6:11–12; cf. 30:2, 18). He also characterizes the friends' speech as lacking such power (26:2, quoted above). By contrast, Job ascribes this kind of power or ability to God, or to a hypothetical contender with God (9:4, 19; 26:12). Beyond this abstraction, the monsters and Job share an entire vocabulary of the body. Bones and sinews form a parallel pair in descriptions of Behemoth and of Job:

יחפץ זנבו כמו־ארז
גיד פחדיו ישרגו
עצמיו אפיקי נחושה
גרמיו כמטיל ברזל

    His tail arches like a cedar;
    The thews of his thighs intertwine.
    His bones are tubes of bronze,
    His gristles like iron bars. (40:17–18)

---

71. Newsom, *Job*, 250, 251.

Job is made of the same stuff, but merely of skin, flesh, and bones (10:11). Unlike Behemoth's bones, Job's are far more vulnerable (19:20a; 30:17a). And unlike Job's wasted bones, Behemoth's are like bronze and iron. Where else do we find metals? They occur in the wisdom poem, on a list of strong and mysterious things that come from the earth (28:2). The language of Behemoth's body thus has two referents, one to Job and one to the wisdom hymn. The references to Job are contrasts, and those to hidden and difficult things, similarities.

Another common pool of terms is used for Behemoth's and Job's surroundings, and again, the same terms set up contrasts. The root שׂחק, "play, sport, mock," denotes a pleasant pastoral home for Behemoth where animal companions sport around him (40:20). Job, on the other hand, is the target of hostile sport (12:4; 30:1). Further, Job is surrounded (סבב) by attacking bowmen (16:13), but Behemoth is surrounded by shade. The latter term occurs in contrasts of its own: Behemoth rests in pleasant shade (צלל), but darkness encompasses Job (7:2; 17:7). Job's surroundings contrast with Behemoth's as sharply as his substance does with the monster's powerful body. Yet these contrasts are articulated through a common vocabulary.

Thus Newsom's contention that Behemoth resembles Job is problematic. Given the presence of so many terms (my discussion here is not exhaustive) in the Behemoth description that are applied elsewhere to Job, it seems clear that the poet alludes to earlier passages. However, the same terms do not have the same semantic or emotional valence when applied to each figure. How to explain this? The easiest explanation may be that Behemoth is much stronger and more magnificent than Job, and Job is supposed to take some lesson from this. Such an explanation falls into the binary scheme of theodicy, and depicts God making a point that no one was arguing. I suggest instead that the divine speech draws on the same terms that Job used of himself precisely in order to re-describe the monstrous as magnificent. This new description, with new valences for old terms, would apply to Job as well as to Behemoth. After all, Job has not only been attacked, he has also withstood an attack.

The attack motifs reappear in the description of Leviathan, only now, all attempted attacks fail. The description of Leviathan thus provides an opposite number to the successful attack on Job (16:12–16). Leviathan's body resists arrows, does not break or bend, withstands everything Job cannot. As bodies under attack, then, Job and Leviathan are very different. Might there also be a way in which Job resembles Leviathan? He has characterized the friends' and others' ridicule of him as a kind of attack, and this he does withstand. Job contrasts the power of his words with the impotence of the friends' words. In his self-representation, if not in his body, Job's power stands on par with Leviathan's. Again, New-som's observation that Leviathan resembles God is valid, but needs nuance. Leviathan's description draws on a set of terms that are shared with Job and God. There is a family resemblance among them. In the monsters, the monstrous, in which both Job and God participate, has been rendered sublime. By contrast, the friends' normalizing discourse, if successful, would render both God and Job tame—and banal. Job's speeches could only discover the terms, but could not wield them in this way.

*What Monsters Do*
What effect does this display have on Job, and on a reader? These are separate questions. It is time to return to Steiner's characterization of the speeches as an aesthetic response to a moral question. Among biblical scholars, the most prominent advocates for some kind of aesthetic under-standing of the speeches have been Gordis, Good, and Newsom. Gordis argued that the speeches demonstrate God's joy in the beauty of creation, and that the proper human response for Job and for readers is to have faith in the moral order of the universe based on our perception of the aesthetic order:

> The vivid and joyous description of nature is not an end in itself: it under-scores the insight that nature is not merely a mystery, but is also a miracle, a cosmos, a thing of beauty. From this flows the basic conclusion at which the poet has arrived: *just as there is order and harmony in the natural world, though imperfectly grasped by man, so there is order and meaning in the moral sphere, though often incomprehensible to man...* The beauty of the world becomes an anodyne to man's suffering.[72]

I have three objections to Gordis's view. The first is philosophical: it is by no means clear that there is any logical relationship between aesthetic and moral order. Perhaps this is why Gordis has to assert the connection and require faith in the "mystery" of a relation between beauty and justice. Gordis recommends that Job and the reader take beauty as a warrant for ignoring the moral question. By contrast, Steiner has raised the question precisely and without obfuscating mysteries: *does* an aes-thetic response answer a moral question? Saying yes without saying how does not help us. My second objection is a matter of practical literary criticism. The poem does not seem to backpedal away from the dialogue in this manner. As Good aptly observed, "Yahweh's case for the divine power has no necessary ingredient of the moral in it, and, indeed, the

72. Gordis, *God and Man*, 133 (emphasis original).

3. *Figures*                                              97

question in 40.8 points precisely away from structuring the universe in
moral terms, of righteousness and wickedness, innocence and guilt, and
toward power, annulling 'order' or its obverse."[73] Finally, it seems to me
that Gordis trivializes both moral and aesthetic experience by calling
beauty an "anodyne" for suffering.[74] From a moral perspective, this term
suggests that God can inflict pain for no reason if God also provides
some aspirin. But the moral question is whether a just God can inflict
pain for no cause, regardless of what happens later. As for aesthetics, it is
undeniable that art objects can be used as analgesics. Such a view treats
art, even the art of cosmic order, as something added to a basic structure
that is not fundamentally aesthetic. Gordis does not state this explicitly,
but the fact that he refers our perception of natural harmony back to the
moral realm and to propositions about God's nature implies that the
function of art is thus secondary and dependent on these more fundamental structures. The deeper question is whether the basic order and
meaning of the cosmos is *primarily* aesthetic, and if so, what sort of
human response is appropriate.

Thus Gordis introduces an aesthetic dimension without taking it seriously. Good's reading, on the other hand, clears the way for an aesthetic
approach to the divine speeches. He argues that the dialogue has set up a
zero-sum universe, in which morality must be balanced with reward,
immorality with punishment. This assumption makes it impossible for
both God and Job to be right. However, the divine speeches are ironic
demolitions of this view. God's attitude toward the monsters is deeply
ambivalent: even if he can control them, it is not clear that such control is
easy.[75] For Good, then, the irony of the divine speeches undermines the
ethical structures proposed in the dialogue; a cosmic order with no
indication of moral structure has been displayed; and Job's encounter
with God brings him an almost Socratic wisdom of knowing that he did
not know (which is far more than the friends know). I find much to
admire in his view that Job repents of repentance and gives up this sort
of religion.[76] Good's discussion is refreshing because it emphasizes the
ambiguities in the text in order to free it from the vice-grip of moralizing
interpretations, and it saves Job from a second naiveté that would really
amount to a capitulation that is not honest about itself. Nevertheless,
Good has not pushed his aesthetic insight as far as it could go.

73. Good, *Tempest*, 369.
74. I sense that Newsom (*Job*, 253) also finds this term irritating.
75. Good, *Tempest*, 364–65.
76. The phrase "repent of repentance" appears in ibid., 377, but the discussion
leading up to it runs through pp. 375–77.

The strongest statement of what sort of aesthetic experience is at stake, and what its implication are, comes from Newsom. She argues for an understanding based on Longinus's concept of the tragic sublime.[77] Specifically, the two qualities of the sublime which she finds in the book of Job are the jolt out of self-possession, and identification with the author of the sublime. I find Newsom's analysis persuasive for a reader, but not for Job the character and the transformation he undergoes. I will argue that Job does indeed experience a self-forgetfulness, for which he asked in the dialogue. However, I do not find the second phase of sublime transport in Job himself. Longinus is writing about readers or hearers in relation to works of art that do not represent their own experience. Job does not have the necessary distance from himself, nor should he.

A better classical analogy to Job can be found in George Walsh's discussion of Odysseus at the Phaeacian court (*Od.* 8). In the passage, Odysseus is incognito, a guest at a banquet. The singer who provides the evening's entertainment performs a poem about the Trojan War and its heroes. While the hosts enjoy the performance, Odysseus weeps. Walsh observes that the hosts and their guest are essentially different audiences for this song:

> Only Odysseus has direct experience of the events commemorated in the song; the Phaeacians (like us) contemplate the deeds of heroes from a great distance, for they will never achieve anything heroic themselves. These two audiences bring different expectations to the performance... The song itself, the transformation of experience into art, has not diminished the pain of recollection; no healing distance separates experience from its poetic representation.[78]

Similarly, Job, in relation to the divine speeches, and the reader, in relationship to the book of Job, are distinct audiences. The same aesthetic analysis cannot be applied to both, for Job is too involved in his own experience and in its representation. For him as for Odysseus, there is no healing distance. There is, however, a crucial difference: unlike Odysseus, Job has been the poet of his own suffering, and the representation of his suffering does become an aesthetic mode of experiencing it. The question, then, is how the divine speeches alter Job's experience while respecting the integrity of his self-representation.

---

77. Newsom, *Job*, 253–55. The relevant passage in Longinus is from *On The Sublime*, I. 2.

78. George B. Walsh, *The Varieties of Enchantment: Early Greek Views of the Nature and Function of Poetry* (Chapel Hill: University of North Carolina Press, 1984), 3–4.

The two speeches, taken together, enact a rhetorical shift from theodicy to aesthesis. Each begins with a brief display of divine chest-thumping (38:2–5; 40:7–14). If one stops at that and takes theodicy alone to be the issue, then the speeches sound like a display of divine power, nothing more. There are, however, cues indicating that something else is going on. To put it colloquially, is God saying "Look at me!" or "Look at *that*!"? The first speech indeed lends itself to the "Look at me" understanding, but leaves the second speech unexplained and largely inexplicable. The second option—"Look at *that*"—explains the presence of the monsters and also provides the speeches, especially the second one, with a rhetorical function beyond mere repetition of what was never at issue. Taken together, the speeches effect a change in Job's attention, something for which he has asked (9:27–28).

As many commentators have noted, the first divine speech focuses on the cosmic order. The human realm is ignored for the sake of the big picture: phenomena of the sea, earth, and air, birth and death, and some very strange animals. The constant refrain "Do you know?" harps on Job's ignorance compared to God's knowledge, and yet the elaboration of cosmic order and strange animals tends to direct the attention away from both God and Job, and toward the strangeness of the cosmos itself. In particular, one pointed question refers back to Job's first speech:

> Have you entered the springs of the sea,
> Walked in the recesses of the deep?
> Have Death's Gates been revealed to you,
> Have you seen the dark portals?
> Have you examined the earth's expanse,
> Tell, if you know all this. (38:16–18; cf. 3:5–9)

Job did not claim to know Yam and Tehom, but he did compare God's action toward them to God's action toward himself. The comparison did not rest on direct knowledge of these figures, but rather on God's destruction of them in order to create an orderly cosmos. Nevertheless, the author of Job has turned the myths on their heads: these monstrous figures were not destroyed and removed from the cosmic order, but rather remain as essential constituents of that order. To be sure, the shift is not complete in the first speech; the elaboration of bizarre creatures, captivating as it is, does not fully shift the grounds of Job's identification with such things. Nor does the rhetoric fully shift attention away from God and Job and the whole situation.

Let us consider the shift in form that occurs over the pair of speeches. In the first speech, the rhetorical questions begin with "Do you know?" (various forms of ידע, at 38:5, 33; 39:1, 2). This is familiar territory from the dialogue, for it implies the superiority of God's knowledge to Job's. Rhetorical questions about Job's knowledge alternate with other question forms: who? where? when? can? Indeed, "Do you know?" is confined to the first half of the first speech; the second half gives way to modal questions, that is, imperfects that question Job's ability to do this or that. Good notes that the divine tone is sarcastic and highlights Job's limitations.[79] To leave it at that would be to portray God as vaunting over something Job did not claim, and Good does not leave it at that. He goes on to suggest that the first speech opens up the larger cosmos in which Job's suffering occurs, demonstrates the divine power from God's point of view, and, most important, leaves a far more complex picture than either Job or his friends have imagined:

> Yahweh's apparently single-minded self-glorification portrays an ambiguous world, whose order contains disorder, whose disorder undermines the order. Both stem from a mind that scoffs at the limitations of the mere human who "darkens counsel" by "ignorant words." Insofar as the "counsel" signifies cosmic design, the ambiguity of simultaneous order and disorder seems to darken itself in the deity's own words.[80]

This ambiguity sets the stage for the second speech, in which the sense of an agent for all the modal verbs becomes so ambiguous as to be indeterminate. "Do you know?" is gone, and "Can you?" recedes into "Who can?" which in turn yields the ground to the monsters themselves. After vv. 1–6, ch. 41 abandons the rhetorical questions in favor of indicative statements about Behemoth and Leviathan. The monsters are now center stage, not as primordial agents who have been destroyed but as astonishing presences in the cosmos.

Job's responses to the divine rehearsal are famously terse. How one reads them depends a great deal on what one thinks the issues are between God and Job. If we take theodicy to be the main issue, God has brow-beaten Job either into a sullen silence or into a complete self-abasement. What more is there to say if God only relentlessly insists on his power and ignores the moral question? But if we realize that it was Bildad, and not Job, who asked "Does God pervert justice?" then we should question whether the speeches are an answer to this question. What, in contrast to the friends, has Job asked? Job asked for God to appear and show him his sins; God has, and the speeches find no fault with him. (The declaration that Job has spoken well occurs in the epilogue.) Job also asked to forget himself, and his reply to God indi-

---

79. Good, *Tempest*, 344–45.
80. Ibid., 348.

cates his own insignificance. In this sense, Job's response to the speeches fit the first phase of the sublime, loss of self-possession. Here we have a fit between what Job said in dialogue, the divine speeches, and Job's reply. In the first reply, Job's line "I am small" raises the question, compared to what? Not to God; he never claimed to be commensurate with God. If this is a shift in perspective and not a repetition of what has already been aired, Job is comparing himself to the cosmic order to which God has directed his attention. The divine speech thus responds to Job's desire for self-forgetfulness; the reply indicates that he now sees himself in a much larger context, a context which enables a measure of self-forgetfulness.

But does he experience the second phase of the sublime—the feeling that one has composed the words or work oneself? If this is the case, the response should indicate some feeling for having created Behemoth and Leviathan, or at least the poems about them. Let us consider the second response (42:2–6) in the context of monster imagery (42:3): "I talked of things I did not know, / Wonders beyond my ken." The term נפלאות should be taken as a reference to what Job has just heard and visualized: Behemoth and Leviathan. The root appears several times in the book and always indicates the wondrous and uncanny things in the cosmos. In 9:10, it occurs after several verses referring to the primordial monstrous elements of the sea, wind, and constellations. There, it functions almost as a cypher, a place-holder for everything that lies beyond human comprehension. The context and meaning are similar in Elihu's speech (37:5): heavenly theophanies such as thunder and lightening both specify the wonders and point beyond what can be articulated. However, the root פלא occurs in an unusual form in one more context. Job says of God's action toward him:

ותשב תתפלא־בי

You demonstrate your wondrousness through me again and again (Job 10:16).[81]

The verse appears among images of hunting and attacking. Job thus represents the divine attack in his body as an enactment of divine wonders. In Job's second reply, then, the term נפלאות carries the weight of these earlier uses: the inexplicable and the violent are manifestations of God. In 10:16, Job (ironically, bitterly) classified himself as one of God's "wonders." In the second response, I suggest that he follows the divine re-valuation of the monstrous. Perhaps now he has placed himself in the

81. The translation is mine.

divine menagerie, rather than in the tidy human social world. Within this monstrous company, he does not stand out.[82]

It is common to see Job's responses as a comparison of his knowledge to God's. Since he professes throughout the dialogue that he does not know or understand God, it does not make sense to have him take back something he did not claim. Nor is his response large enough to indicate a sense of authorship over the monsters or the poems about them, as the second phase of sublime transport would require. Interpretation of responses must take into account where Job was, in order to understand where he is. In the dialogue, he compared the divine attack on him to the divine attack on primordial monsters, but insisted that he could not be important enough to warrant the attack. The divine speeches recover chaos monsters as part of creation, and depict the monstrous bodies reconstituted in splendor. Behemoth's description reinterprets Job himself, in that it draws on a common pool of terms but changes their significance. Leviathan is depicted as invulnerable against attack. He is the opposite of Job's body, which cannot withstand attack, but he is also the embodiment of Job's integrity, which holds up under assault from the friends and the human social world. The monsters, then, shift Job's attention away from himself, and yet he is also recovered and transformed as one of God's magnificent monsters. The divine speeches articulate Job even more powerfully than Job himself did, yet they build on rather than demolish his own self-articulation. Aesthetic attention to the monsters brings Job to this insight. Thus he remains the author of his own representation, if not of his suffering; but he is not transported into a sense of authorship over Behemoth, Leviathan, the cosmos, or the poems of these.

*Disability and Aesthetic Transcendence in the Book of Job*
Does this answer the moral question? At the disjunction between moral interpretation and aesthetic reply, disability studies can be particularly useful. I see two major points of continuity between the book of Job and contemporary disability studies. First, disability often becomes a sight of contested descriptions: who articulates the disabled body and its meanings? In *The Rejected Body*, philosopher Susan Wendell concludes her analysis of feminism and disability with some reflections on transcendence of the body.[83] She argues against the view that the real body only reacts to other causes but cannot be a cause on its own. According to

82. I think it is possible to read the *min-* as comparative rather than superlative: "things more wonderful than I am." This does no violence to the grammar, but, to my knowledge, no commentators have suggested this.
83. Wendell, *Rejected Body*, 165–79.

Wendell, the desire to find a moral or spiritual "meaning" in physical suffering denies that the body itself can be a cause. The body can initiate new insights, but these are not of the sort that reconstruct past causes or meanings of the body's pain. For Job, disease and disability are the *beginning* of new insight, rather than the *middle* of a sin-and-repentance narrative, as the friends would have it. There is nothing moral about this. Job refuses to inspire; he is not a well-behaved cripple. Wendell's notion of the body as a cause does not have the ancient Near Eastern metaphysical trappings of the book of Job, but it can serve as a prism through which the conflict between Job and the friends can be seen more clearly: the friends insist on a moral meaning to Job's suffering, and Job says that there is none. His suffering has no moral cause, and no moral conclusion. Job does not ask for an explanation of his suffering, nor for a return to good fortune; undeserved suffering implies that health and wealth are similarly arbitrary. In moral terms, the ending is thus anti-climactic, even obfuscating: although Job's suffering ends and his good fortune is restored, this reversal in no way undoes the harm. Nor would it undo the insight into divinity. But as an aesthetic resolution, it is ironic in the extreme.

Second, disability provides the kind of intractable situation that resists narrative closure. A condition such as chronic pain does not indicate imminent death, nor can it be resolved by any known means. For the person who has it, the problem is how to go on living with it. Forgetfulness, of the body and the self, is both needed and impossible (cf. Job 9:27–28). Here again, Wendell is useful: against postmodern suspicion of the Cartesian self, Wendell argues instead for what could be called embodied transcendence:

> To choose to exercise some habits of mind that distance oneself from chronic, often meaningless physical suffering increases freedom, because it expands the possibilities of experience beyond the miseries and limitations of the body. It is because they increase the freedom of consciousness that I am drawn to calling these strategies of transcendence. It is because we are led to adopt them by the body's pain, discomfort, or difficulty, and because they are ways of interpreting and dealing with bodily experience, that I call them transcendence of the body.[84]

That is, the body both makes itself impossible to ignore and also forces the self to find modes of identification and self-esteem that go beyond the bodily experience. One of these modes is aesthetic perception, which itself focuses the attention on another physical form. We can see a similar process at work in the book of Job. In asking for a divine appearance

84. Ibid., 178.

and for self-forgetfulness, Job has asked how to go on living once one knows that the answer to Bildad's question, "Does God pervert justice?" is Yes. I suggest that the divine speeches can best be understood as an answer to *Job's* question; the response they provide is an aesthetic path to transcendence. This is, I think, what the divine speeches do for Job: they enable him to attain his desired shift of attention away from his own body. But this transcendence is not quite vertical, into a disembodied realm. Over the two speeches, God shifts attention from God's self to creation, especially to the monstrous forms in creation. By the necessary use of physical forms—Behemoth and Leviathan—the aesthetic transcendence retains a bodily dimension. The descriptions of the monsters take up and transform the vocabulary of Job's experience. By the choice of monsters, the speeches draw Job farther along the path on which he has set out, rather than forcing him back into the neat categorizations of the friends.

If this were all, then the book would prove a weak remedy—Gordis's anodyne, the Phaeacians' entertainment at the represented suffering of others. But the conclusion accomplishes more than diverting Job's attention to other forms. The poet has linked Job and the monsters through a common discourse of the body, such that his own experience is taken up within the monstrous. The divine speeches represent God as the artist of Behemoth and Leviathan, and as the poet who hymns them. Within the stated assumptions of the book, God is the maker of Job's body and of its suffering. But who is the poet of Job's self-representation? There are several figures who attempt and fail to represent Job: first the Satan, and then the friends. Interpretations that find fault with Job attempt to override, or over-write, Job's own self-representation by confining the divine speeches to the friends' understanding of the cosmos. What has God said or done about Job's self-representation in speech? His first affirmations of Job's integrity (1:8; 2:3) clearly include behavior, but cannot include the self-representing speeches of the dialogue. Thus God's final affirmation of Job's integrity *and his words* (42:7–8) leaves that self-representation intact. Nothing in the divine speeches has over-written Job's self-narration. I argued above that the language of monstrous bodies is shared in common between Job and the monsters, but valued differently. The full impact of this bodily discourse is a rhetoric that both affirms Job's self-representation (and in so doing, respects his integrity) but also places his own narrative in a cosmic context that alters its significance. Rather than a moral disaster in need of normalization, God presents the monstrous as an aesthetic triumph. Further, much of that narration linked speech about Job with speech about God. The conclusion treats these as all of a piece, and gives primacy to Job's speech about God: "You have not spoken the truth about me as did my servant Job." Articulating the truth of one's self and body is taken up within articulating the truth about God.

We return to Steiner's perplexity: can a moral problem have an aesthetic solution? In one sense, it cannot. The book of Job presents a God who causes human suffering for no other reason than to win a bet with someone whose job is to pick quarrels. Surely this is trivial, and for that reason, the interpretation that God is a sadist can never be decisively eliminated. If the poet of Job does mean to undo the ancient Near Eastern association of cosmic and moral order, and propose that aesthetic order is more fundamental, this move does come at the price of demoting goodness, both ours and God's, to a secondary role. That is, instead of a cosmos of fundamental goodness with art as the analgesic, we have instead a cosmos of fundamental beauty, with goodness as a human social necessity—dare I say, as the analgesic? In this reading, the concluding detail that Job's daughters are beautiful emerges as the final grace note in Job's transformation into the man who begets beauty.

Earlier, I noted that the figure Job and the reader of the book of Job are distinct audiences with distinct aesthetic situations. Job himself is the third possibility that is not present at the Phaeacian court: the human being as author of the representation of his suffering. This is a special condition, for it lacks the distance that enables the audience's straightforward pleasure, but it offers a measure of distance not available to the sufferer in the middle of things. Like Wendell's position of embodied transcendence, Job stands both intimately inside and also above his own experience. What of the reader of the book of Job? Here I would like to amplify Steiner's claim that the book draws the reader through an experience. Some readers experience Job as a sinful and arrogant man who is put in his place. This is to read badly and ignore much. Others experience God as the torturer of an innocent man, and suppose that the poem means to observe that the innocent suffer, and to say nothing more. Had the book ended before the divine speeches, I would find this view persuasive. Given their presence, and the power of their poetry, I as a reader want them to say more and say it better than what Elihu has already said poorly. If the reader remains within the initial moral structures, then all the sublime poetry is for nothing. If one is drawn in by it, another meaning emerges. The poetry itself enacts aesthetic transcendence in the reader by drawing attention away from the initial situation and into wonder at the sublimity of the cosmos. Perhaps the book of Job even implies that abandoning the good for the sublime is worth the bargain, no matter what the cost.

## Disability as Aesthetic Feature

That the book of Job would not be possible without the main character's disabling disease goes without saying; that Genesis would not be possible, or would be unrecognizably different, without female infertility and male blindness, has been less obvious. Thus these texts exemplify narrative prosthesis in the sense that their plots hinge on disability. Mitchell and Snyder see this plot-inducing function as a strange kind of power that must be effaced, if possible. Sometimes the effacement is quite literal, as in the case of a cure, or the disabled character's death. But effacement can be achieved through re-directed attention.

I contend that such re-direction operates significantly in Genesis, and takes the foreground in Job. To read only God's power and fail to perceive that it walks on the crutch of disabled human beings is one kind of misdirection and effacement. Even to the extent that the representations of power compete with representations of benevolence, theodicy can be a misdirection. In both Genesis and Job, God is deeply implicated in the disabling of the human figures. Theodicy asks how a good God can also allow, or even cause, evil and suffering. This problem is, I believe, philosophically insoluble, given its assumption of an all-powerful and all-good God. But why is disability needed, and needed so often, for God to cure, work with or around, or make wagers? The problem is not a conflict between God's goodness and power, but rather between the claim that God is powerful and the representation of God's power so centrally through the disabled human body. In Genesis, the disabled human representationally props up the powerful God, not the other way around. In Job, God seems strangely insecure about whether his power can make it on its own, independent of how a given human body fares.

Another possible re-direction would be the question whether the disabled figure is positive or negative, a hero/heroine or a villain. Against such a line of interpretation, Mitchell and Snyder say that "...the problem of the representation of disability is not the search for a most 'positive' story of disability, as it has often been formulated in disability studies, but rather a thoroughgoing challenge to the undergirding authorization to interpret that disability invites."[85] With respect to the Hebrew Bible, such an approach will be enormously tempting to many exegetes. To be sure, Isaac has probably been a major victim of what Wynn calls "normate hermeneutics"; the representation of his visuality or lack of it is quite nuanced, to the extent that his impairment is not simply good

---

85. Mitchell and Snyder, *Narrative Prosthesis*, 59.

or bad. Disability-Positive Isaac is thus not an objection to my thesis because disability in these books poses the deeper questions suggested by Mitchell and Synder.

In contrast to Genesis, the book of Job allows Job's own competing and compelling self-representation to expose the fissures in this represen- tation of God's power. To be sure, the effacement occurs: in the end, Job is healed, his wealth is restored, and he gets a new family. This ending, to me, comes as an enormous let-down, for how could he go on as if nothing had happened? Or does he? Job, in a way, shifts the playing field to one of aesthetic contest—Job's verbal self-making versus the friends' and even God's—so as to open up that question of who is authorized to interpret disability (or anything else). The difference among interpreta- tions does not lie in *how* one perjures oneself in God's defense, but rather in *whether* one takes this task as the assignment. For those who do not, the man operating the controls behind the curtain, that is, the human author(s) representing a powerful God, suddenly appear in plain sight.

Chapter 4

# RHETORIC:
# THE SENSORY STRUCTURE OF DIVINE–HUMAN
# COMMUNICATION

"Those who are blind fail to see you even when you hold up a mallet or a *hosu*. [Blind to the very core.—This is no other than 'benefiting all beings.'—Not necessarily failing to see.]
"Those who are deaf fail to hear you even when you talk volubly enough. [– Deaf to the very core!—This is no other than 'benefiting all beings.'—Not necessarily altogether deaf.—That something is still unheard.]"

—"Gensha on the Three Invalids"[1]

You deaf, listen,
and you blind, look up and see!
Who is blind if not my servant,
and who is deaf like my messenger whom I send?

—Isa 42:18–19[2]

When a figure bears the disability, and often the narrative profluence along with it, disability nevertheless remains localized. The disabled figure may exert an odd magnetic field, inadvertently influencing other characters or exegetes to alter their behavior and speech. Or not. As Mitchell and Snyder note, in literature as in life, the abled gaze slides over disabilities,[3] as if they were all invisible, except for the perceptual hole where a sight was registered and avoided. I believe this is the case for standard commentary on biblical narratives, where disabled characters are either ignored completely or isolated.[4] When we turn to

---

1.   "Gensha on the Three Invalids," in D. T. Suzuki, *Manual of Zen Buddhism* (New York: Grove, 1960), 120–21.
2.   From Klaus Baltzer, *Deutero-Isaiah: A Commentary on Isaiah 40–55* (Minneapolis: Fortress, 2001), 148.
3.   Mitchell and Snyder, *Narrative Prosthesis*, 50–53.
4.   Schipper has made the definitive case for this omission. *Mephibosheth*, 1–5.

the overtly rhetorical and dialogical genres, disability no longer adheres to isolated figures. Instead, it forms an entire network of representations that no longer represent individual bodies, but communication itself. My case studies come from the book of Psalms, where disability and its opposite (whatever that is in a particular case) inform the dramatic address of one speaker to another party, and from the book of Isaiah, the diverse strata of which pick up disability imagery from each other and amplify it to achieve a totality that represents human–divine communication in a way that no one author ever intended.

### Evoked Potential: The Disabled Body in the Psalms

As poetry, most of the Psalms are dramatic lyrics. In the lyric mode, the poetic discourse is fully identified with a speaker who articulates an experience, to an implied audience that can range from a subtle, uncharacterized presence to a fully characterized addressee. Dramatic lyrics fall on the latter end of this spectrum: the implied audience is a definite persona rather than a subtle presence. Robert Browning's "My Last Duchess" is a classic example of the type. Dramatic lyric is distinguished from the dramatic mode proper in that the other personae are not represented as speakers. They are, however, represented by implication in the single speaker's address. The lyric thus depicts for its (implied) reader both the speaker and the implied audience of the speaker's address. (To be distinguished from the implied audience of the poem; this tension is palpable in "My Last Duchess.") More deeply, dramatic lyric represents the speaker's own self-representation, and also the speaker's implied representation of the addressee.

As dramatic lyrics, then, the Psalms imply God, not just as an existent, but as a characterized other. The speakers represent God, and this representation is inseparable from the speaker's self-representation: the same speech represents both. Just as advertisements, in their attempt to persuade us to buy, already tell us who we are, so do the Psalm speakers tell God who they wish God to be.[5] As prayers, these double representations are addressed to the same party. That is, the speaker represents him-/herself to God, and simultaneously represents God to God's self. Among the varied means of representation, body imagery

---

5. We should distinguish more clearly between "Psalmist" as anonymous author, and the speaker in any given Psalm, just as literary critics maintain a clear distinction between the poet and the speaker of a poem. Even when an author represents her own experience, the speaking voice in the literary work is itself a representation.

is prominent in the Psalms. Recently, Gillmayr-Bucher pointed out the unusual statistical frequency of such imagery and analyzed it from a reader-response perspective.[6] I intend to focus more narrowly on images of illness, injury, and sensory disability. Although these may refer to or be used by persons who are actually sick, or may evoke empathy in the reader, this discussion will consider the use of these images as a means of structuring the dramatic lyric discourse. Specifically, the Psalmist uses images of sickness and disability to articulate a polarity between human impotence and divine power. Paradoxically, however, it is the speaker's disabling self-description that calls out God's power. That is, bodily weakness becomes rhetorical power, with the purpose of leveraging God into action.

These images are scattered widely throughout the Psalms. Even if we isolate the Psalms in which they are clustered, they will not all be of the same form-critical genre. As one might expect, psalms of individual lament are well-represented, but other forms appear too. In the interest of brevity, I will discuss in detail Pss 38 and 94, in which images of illness and disability are clustered. Psalm 38 is an individual lament, but Ps 94 is harder to classify. It combines features of communal lament and communal thanksgiving, but has a prominent individual voice and hymn-like qualities. Close reading of these will reveal nuanced dynamics of representation. As a second angle on the problem, I will consider the use of one term—חלה—and a few of its related terms as they appear in a variety of Psalm contexts. Thus, my strategy falls far short of comprehensiveness. I seek instead to demonstrate what might be done from a disability perspective with the entire collection of Psalms. My two-pronged approach reveals a pervasive strategy of Psalmist dramatic lyric: the use of disability to evoke power.

*Psalm 38: A Subtle Lament*
Psalm 38 is a psalm of lament, with a strong first-person voice throughout.[7] It includes the standard three figures of the speaker, enemies, and God. Further, it abounds in images of bodily injury, illness, and disability. If one reads through the lens of illness equals sin, these images

---

6.  Susanne Gillmayr-Bucher, "Body Images in the Psalms," *JSOT* 28 (2004): 301–21. Her analysis of the imagery does not distinguish generic body images from images of injury, illness, or disability. The thesis is that the vivid imagery leads a reader to bring his/her own bodily experience to the reading.

7.  That is, it is not a dialogic lament as described by Carleen Mandolfo in *God in the Dock: Dialogic Tension in Psalms of Lament* (Sheffield: Sheffield Academic Press, 2002).

appear static and univocal.[8] Psalm 38 does indeed include references to both sin and illness/disability, but the structure of the association is not stable. The opening strophe begins with a request for God not to be angry, and a representation of a body under divine attack (vv. 2–4). The rhetoric moves from a request not to be rebuked, to an attribution of a current situation to God, and finally to a pair of strong negative existentials that express a total condition as a result of some sin. The last statements are so all-encompassing that they seem not to leave room for the further action that the speaker is asking God not to take. Further, the causal use of מפני is ambiguous between a temporal sense (first sin, then illness) and a mutually exclusive sense (health and sin cannot co-exist). If the psalm-speaker means to express the view that sin is the cause of illness, one would expect this association to remain stable, and the requested remedy would be forgiveness and then health. However, illness and disability do not remain stable signifiers of sin. As the poem proceeds, the significance of an ill and disabled body shifts several times.

The opening strophe is followed by two units that juxtapose the speaker's ravaged body with two contrasting audiences. Verses 5–8 depict a speaker stripped of bodily and emotional health: wounds fester, loins burn, flesh is unsound (unhealthy), and the body is crushed. The physical descriptions are interlaced with severe emotional distress: constant mourning, heartache, and self-castigation for the speaker's own responsibility (v. 5). These descriptions are not presented in a vacuum; rather, the next strophe places the speaker's body before two audiences, God and friends. Verse 10 asserts that God knows the speaker's distress. This is not simply a wish or statement of faith. God as the audience is strongly contrasted with the social audience of friends, who avoid the speaker. Indeed, the parallelism of vv. 11–12 suggests that failing strength and sight are metaphors of social abandonment. On the level of literal representation, these lines depict a common pattern of shunning someone who is sick or

8. Frederik Lindstrom, in *Suffering and Sin: Interpretations of Illness in the Individual Complaint Psalms* (Stockholm: Almqvist & Wiksell International, 1994), argues that the individual lament Psalms treat sickness as the experience of God's withdrawn presence, without postulating sin as the cause of sickness. Ps 38 is an apparent exception. He suggests that this motif in the current text is a product of editorial addition, and that the original psalm did not equate sickness with sin. I find his case convincing, but have a strong preference for analyzing the text we have rather than reconstructions of which we cannot be certain. In either case, the dramatic-lyric function of the images is the same.

disabled.[9] Within the verses, 11a is parallel to 11b—heart throbs/
strength fails/light is gone—and 12a is parallel to 12b—friends and
companions stand aloof/neighbors stand far off. Read thus sequen-
tially, others have abandoned the speaker because of his afflictions.
But if we note that the parallelism extends over the two verses, with
heart–strength as subjects parallel to friends–companions, and failing
parallel to standing aloof, and similarly with the b versets, this strophe
also suggests that social abandonment *is* the loss of strength and
sight.[10] The polysemy of these verses provides the foundation for later
modulations of the images' meaning.

The next segment, vv. 13–16, builds upon the injured speaker in
relation to contrasting audiences, and it significantly shifts the valuation of disability images. Not only have friends abandoned the speaker,
but enemies are actively plotting harm (v. 13). In response, the speaker
declares, "But I am like the deaf, I do not hear; Like the mute, who
cannot speak" (v. 14; v. 15 continues the images of deafness and muteness). Do these images indicate further abasement, adding deafness
and muteness to injury, as it were?[11] On the contrary, the tone of complaint is lacking here. Deafness and muteness are presented as the
*correct* response to the enemies.[12] The rationale appears in vv. 16–17.
First, God is the party who must answer, not the speaker. Thus deafness and muteness are the speaker's appropriate role. Second, in v. 17,
the speaker prays only that the enemies do not rejoice or boast over
him/her. I suggest that we think of this situation as one of competing

9. Wendell (*Rejected Body*, 129–33) remarks how disabled persons often find
social shunning worse than the disability itself. Contrast Craigie's remark on vv.
12–21: "Whereas the first consequence of sickness is to create a sense of guilt
and distance from God, as in v3–11, the second consequence is the development
of a sense of alienation from fellow human beings, as described in these verses.
The alienation may be partly paranoia and partly real…" Such a comment places
the responsibility for social alienation entirely on the sick person, and ignores any
moral responsibility borne by others. Far from a contemporary whim, the psalm
itself holds shunners and mockers responsible for their actions. Peter C. Craigie,
*Psalms 1–50* (Columbia: Thomas Nelson, 2004), 300–306.
10. Richard J. Clifford, in *Psalms 1–72* (Nashville: Abingdon, 2002), 194,
comments, "The Psalmist mourns the loss of health and social standing." But the
Psalm does not treat these as two distinct things; they are intimately related.
11. Lindstrom (*Suffering and Sin*, 247–48) reads these verses this way, as a
continuation of the images in the first strophe.
12. Rashi seems to read this way: confronted with insults, Israel is to act deaf
and not dignify the assailants with a response. See Mayer I. Gruber, *Rashi's
Commentary on Psalms* (Leiden: Brill, 2004), 320

speech acts: the speaker wants to avoid becoming the butt of the enemies' speech act. If that happens, then the speaker is signified by the enemies, that is, he becomes what they say he is. In invoking God, the speaker is calling on another speaker to signify the speaker's value against the enemies. In this context, deafness becomes a way of eluding the speech of others, and muteness relieves one of having to respond.[13] Perhaps it would help to imagine these speech acts spatially: the speaker is using deafness and muteness to place himself/herself above the enemies, not below them, where they could do further harm. Their speech is thus rendered too impotent to require an answer, not too powerful to be answered.

Not too powerful to be answered by God, that is. The speaker's self-representation as a deaf-mute has two implied audiences and different valuations relative to these audiences. In contrast to deaf-muteness as the powerful response to the human enemies, it is self-abasing with respect to God. In vv. 18–19, the speaker confesses his sin and impotence to God. He then asks not for restored health, but for help against the enemies' unjust attacks. The statement that the enemies have returned evil for good, with precisely the motive of attacking a good person, does not cohere well with the confession. It also undermines the explanation for the images of illness: perhaps the enemies have attacked the speaker, and the imagery is a description of the results. A stable reading could be achieved if the enemies were working for God, but the Psalm does not entertain this possibility.

I suggest that the psalm-speaker is not interested in causality. Instead, these verses articulate a concept of proper power. The speaker's powerlessness opens up the space in which God is to manifest God's power. Self-abasement before God, then, is paradoxically powerful: the speaker's weakness calls out God's power against the enemies. Thus the speaker's power with respect to both God and the enemies lies in his/her weakness, as represented by images of illness and disability. The difference between the two implied audiences is that weakness is represented as a refusal of discourse with respect to the enemies, but as a precondition of discourse with respect to God. Illness and disability are not static states; rather they both represent relationships to other parties and generate the very relationships that

13. Kraus' remark that the speaker refrains from speaking to show that he trusts in God seems over-simple: it misses the significant element of competing speech acts and ignores the frankly manipulative quality of the need to jolt God into action. Hans-Joachim Kraus, *Psalms 1–59* (trans. Hilton C. Oswald; Minneapolis: Fortress, 1993), 300–306.

are represented. The speaker's self-representation as ill, disabled, and powerless sets the stage for the conclusion inviting God to intervene (vv. 22–23).[14]

### Psalm 94: Planting the Senses

A similar representation with respect to two audiences occurs in Ps 94. This is a psalm of another sort. Here, there is little ambiguity about why the people are hurt, or whether the enemies are acting on God's behalf. This psalm is a confident demand for divine redress against oppressors. Like Ps 38, it uses images of disability with several different valuations. In all cases, these images do far more than provide vivid detail for a reader's imagination; they structure the discourse between the speaker and other parties. The psalm can be broken down as follows:

1. invocation and petition to God for action (vv. 1–3)
2. description of the people's oppression at the hands of powerful enemies (vv. 4–7)
3. direct address to the enemies (vv. 8–11)
4. direct address to God (vv. 12–13)
5. third-person description of God's action (vv. 14–17)
6. direct address to God (vv. 18–20)
7. third-person affirmation of confidence in God (vv. 21–23)

The images of bodily harm first appear in the second strophe (vv. 4–7). Here, a nested structure begins with a description of the enemies' words, details the physical harm done (crushing, murdering), and concludes with the enemies' speech, this time in direct discourse. At first, a reader might think that the enemies' "boast" expresses their power over the oppressed people. After all, that is what the actions depicted in vv. 5–6 amply demonstrate. But the direct discourse boasts against God, and represents God as blind and unperceptive. Thus the enemies' representation of an impotent God provides their warrant for unjust actions.

The question is, whose speech about God accurately represents God? In the third strophe, the speaker enters into a competitive discourse with the enemies over just this question. The speaker re-depicts the enemies, attributing to them the lack of perception that they have

14. Lindstrom has argued that the individual complaint Psalms as a whole do not view sickness as a result of sin (Lindstrom, *Suffering and Sin*, 6–7). He proposes an editorial process for Ps 38, which could be an exception to his thesis (pp. 445–56). However, if he is correct in general, I hope that I have suggested how else the imagery of sickness may be functioning.

attributed to God. In defense of God's perceptive abilities, the speaker asserts God's creative power over human hearing and sight:

> He who planted the ear, does he not hear?
> He who formed the eye, does he not see? (94:9)[15]

None of this will have much punch unless God acts. Thus, from these straightforward references to the senses, the speaker modulates into a parallel construction in which instruction is the simple quality similar to the ear and the eye, and chastisement is the superlative parallel to the divine powers of sight or hearing. The strophe concludes with an assertion of divine omniscience of human thought (v. 11). Throughout both strophes, perceptive capacities are highly valued as powerful, and their impairments are devalued as indications of impotence. At issue is merely the correct attribution of qualities to figures.

Again, the matter of attribution is the static dimension of a dynamic discourse. Just as the enemies' speech provided a warrant for action, so does the speaker's; but the speaker is explaining God's *inactions*, not his own actions. God, however, has not acted in the time represented in the psalm. Without actions to back up the words, the speaker's assertions are meaningless. How will God be induced to act? Unlike Ps 38, this psalm has little of the distressed plea about it. It begins by requesting divine action in the imperative mode, and concludes in the indicative mode. In spite of this apparently drastic difference in tone, a similar strategy can be discerned in the use of body imagery. The speaker presents God with two rhetorical situations. First, the plight of the people and the speaker's own recollection of individual distress are presented in direct discourse to God. In both cases, the human weakness is represented as the occasion for exercises of divine power. As in Ps 38, the speaker uses the presentation of weakness, illness, and disability, as a *powerful*, that is, effective, way of invoking God. Embedded within the first direct address is the enemies' speech (v. 7). This quotation directly challenges God's power; by repeating it in a speech addressed to God, the speaker both passes on the challenge and implies that God must respond to it. By quoting it, however, the speaker can distance him-/herself from a direct challenge. The possibility that God either might not be powerful, or might choose not to exercise power (which amounts to the same thing for the oppressed

---

15. Cf. Exod 4:11. The whole trope resembles Ps 59, where hostile speakers justify themselves by asserting that no one (powerful) will hear their speech (v. 7). This Psalm represents God responding with some sound of his own: laughter (v. 8).

parties) thus constitutes God as powerful. The second rhetorical situation appears in the speaker's address to the enemies (vv. 8–11). Against the enemies' words and deeds, the speaker has placed his own words asserting God's awareness and power. Ostensibly a challenge to the enemies, it is also a challenge to God to act in accordance with the words. This strategy also relies on the paradoxical disclaimer of one's own power as the means of bringing power to bear on one's own behalf. In short, the speaker is signifying God in telling God who to be and how to act.[16]

## Falling on Deaf Ears

Whether this rhetoric is common to the Psalms' dramatic lyric representation remains to be seen. Although the Psalms are rife with body imagery, one sense in particular plays a prominent role in the dynamics of lyric address to an implied audience, and that is hearing. No one psalm sustains these images for any great length, but the roots for hearing, deafness, and the ear occur 32 times in the Psalms, often with two or three occurrences in the same psalm.[17] The verb שמע is frequent throughout the corpus, but the disproportionate occurrences of חרש in Psalms indicates that hearing and not hearing are a special concern for Israelite religious dramatic lyric. Further, I contend that these terms, like the imagery of disability in Pss 38 and 94, are not merely representative of a static state, or simply the closest metaphor to hand. Rather, they play an active role in the speaker's evocation of God— and not God as a static being with a stable set of properties, but rather God as an unpredictable being whose responses the speaker attempts to govern with a subtle and paradoxical rhetorical strategy.

An analysis of the occurrences of שמע and חרש reveal an interesting contrast. If we isolate only those uses when the term is predicated of

16. There are suggestive connections between Ps 94 and Ps 115. Ps 94 uses the term הבל to denigrate all human thought (94:11). This is the same term used frequently of idols, albeit not in Ps 115. More important, Ps 115 has similar qualities of offering a description (representation) of God as the persuasive tactic to get God to act. This psalm-speakers description of idols as disabled, discussed in Chapter 2, rhetorically counters the nations' question of where Israel's God is (115:2). Thus, two competing human speeches represent Israel's God, with the psalm-speaker employing rhetorical power to evoke a divine response.

17. שמע 19 times, חרש 10 times, and אזן 3 times. The frequency of חרש is remarkable. Including all of its forms and meanings, it occurs a total of 54 times in the biblical corpus, and 10 times in Psalms. That is, nearly one fifth of its occurrences (18.5%) are in Psalms. The book of Isaiah runs second, with 8 occurrences (14.8%).

God, שמע occurs overwhelmingly in positive statements that God hears or has heard.[18] Once, there is a rhetorical question whether God will hear (94:9, quoted above). Also once, the speaker requests that God hear (26:7). The indicative mode is by far the most common. With חרש, however, the case is reversed: of six occurrences in which the term is joined to God in some way, five are negatived imperatives ("Don't be deaf").[19] Only one is indicative, and it is negatived (50:3). This difference raises the question, if Psalm speakers are so sure that God will hear, why do they have to ask God not to be deaf (or mute, depending on the context)?[20]

To answer this question, we must examine the contexts. I count two clear cases in which חרש means and should be translated as "be deaf." In Ps 28:1, the opening invocation reads, "To you, Lord, I call; my rock, do be deaf for me" (28:1a).[21] The speaker then states that God's silence will abandon the speaker to the pit. The parallelism makes the meaning of "deaf" clear. In the second case, the request forms part of the conclusion: "Hear my prayer, Lord, and to my cry, give ear; do not keep silent, do not be deaf" (39:13).[22] Once again, the term is parallel with שמע. When the Psalmist asks God not to be deaf, he/she implies that God can be deaf if God wants. In making this request, the speaker does not imply an unchosen or permanent disability on God's part, but rather power that can exercise deafness as an option. The valuation of deafness is thus ambiguous, depending on *whose* deafness it is. Predicated of arrogant human beings, it is wrong; predicated of supplicant human beings, it is ambivalent; and predicated of God, it is powerful.

In two cases, חרש probably means "be mute, be silent." In Ps 35, the term occurs in the middle of the poem. The speaker has just described enemies' mocking words against him/her, and then declares: "You have seen, O Lord; do not be silent!" (35:22a, NRSV). Here, both meanings are plausible. Given the context, the speaker might be asking God not to be deaf to the enemies' speech, but to hear it and respond; or he/she could be directly asking for God not to fail to speak

18. Pss 6:10; 22:25; 34:7, 18; 55:18, 20; 61:6; 78:5.
19. Pss 28:1; 35:22; 39:13; 83:2; 109:1. All of these are Qal forms.
20. It is revealing that modern translators are shy of this term; neither NRSV nor JPS translate חרש as "deaf" when the term is used of God, even when negatived. However, it clearly means this in at least two cases, is ambiguous in two, and clearly means "be mute, keep silent" in the remaining two. KJV shows a similar reluctance, but the Orthodox Stone edition does use the blunt term "deaf" when appropriate.
21. My translation.
22. My translation.

in response to the enemies. Either sense of חרשׁ would impede the
speaker's vindication. I favor "be mute, be silent" in this context
because vv. 23–24 depict God arguing a case against the enemies.
Hearing is thus assumed, and speech is what must be called forth. This
is a context in which it would be best to retain all of the senses indicated by the Hebrew verb. Unfortunately, an English translator must
choose. In the remaining cases (Pss 50:3; 83:2; 109:1), the sense "be
mute, keep silent" is clearly indicated. In 83:2, for instance, חרשׁ is
one verb among three in a triple parallel construction, and the other
two mean "to be quiet." In all of these cases, the situation to which the
speaker directs God's attention is the speech of enemies. It makes
perfect sense to combat speech with speech that evokes still more
powerful speech.[23]

In either case, the possibility of a divine disability is proposed in its
very denial.[24] No matter which impaired function is warded off in
particular passages, the rhetorical strategy is the same: the speaker is
asking God not to חרשׁ, however we translate it. Just as the request
implied in some contexts that deafness was a possible option, so it
implies that muteness is an option in others.[25] It is significant that the
Psalms only use the stative verb in reference to God, thus indicating
that חרשׁ is depicted as a deliberately chosen action. The substantive-
adjectival form appears only twice in the Psalm corpus, once of the
human speaker (Ps 38:14–15, discussed above), and once of the evil
adder whose example should not be followed (Ps 58:5).[26] In fact, the
usage is completely parallel to the common psalmist request that God
not hide God's face. Whether the image is of a disability (deafness,
muteness) or a physical movement that refuses communication, the
speaker acknowledges the possibility of not being heard. On its face,
this tactic appears simply self-effacing: the speaker acknowledges
his/her own dependence and impotence by admitting that God can do
whatever God wants. However, the artifice of this tactic is that it

23. Strangely, perhaps, there is less distance here between the Hebrew sense
and the translations, although I note that translators prefer "keep/be silent" to "be
mute."

24. Some of this language is too reminiscent of the family member who,
confronted with evidence of a loved one's hearing loss, replies, "She's not deaf!"
and then calls upon the person in question to demonstrate some hearing.

25. Hebrew חרשׁ and Greek κωφός both group deafness and muteness under a
single concept.

26. As noted above, Ps 115 paints an unflattering portrait of idols, including
their multiple physical disabilities. But their inability to hear is expressed using
שׁמע and אזן.

conceals its own evocative power. By suggesting the kind of God that the speaker does not want God to be, he/she evokes the desired God.

As with the sustained images of disability, so with the sporadic uses of hearing and deafness: these terms go beyond literal or metaphorical representation of anything and instead actively generate the implied audience of the dramatic discourse. As speech acts, this strategy is no different from praising someone in order to elicit the praised behavior, or saying that someone is not X in order to induce them not to be X. The paradox, however, cuts in opposite ways in the two situations I have discussed. In Pss 38 and 94, the speaker's self-representation of illness and disability generates the space into which divine power is to step. In the uses of שמע and חרש, on the other hand, the speaker represents God's option to enact disability, in order to evoke the opposite response. In both cases, images of disability are deployed not simply to depict a state that is valued negatively, but as representations of a whole range of communicative options, in which the terms actively elicit some responses and seek to repress others.

*No Soundness in It: Disability as Media in Isaiah*

The canonical book of Isaiah is a composite of three major strata and many complications. Its earliest material would go back to the eighth-century prophet, Isaiah of Jerusalem, and its latest material was composed well after the exile. Although major disjunctions are clear, the editorial process nevertheless produced a document with sustained themes, verbal allusions, and inter-related ideas. Disability imagery occurs frequently in the book, clustered in the exilic portions but with echoes throughout. Its uses are as profligate as the book's editorial history: in Isaiah, disability terms can be positive or negative; literal, metaphorical, or indeterminate; grounded in prophetic eschatology or with incipient apocalyptic significance. My analysis shall focus on the major passages, to demonstrate how disability imagery represents possible modes of divine–human communication. Most of the imagery is metaphorical and not about actual disabled persons. Quite a lot of Isaiah's blind and deaf people have Normal eyes and ears; sometimes, God chooses symbolic disability; and the prophetic speaker deploys disability imagery to represent his mission and role. Given this rich and varied use of language referring to disability, an over-emphasis on the question of healing fails to grasp how deeply these images structure the prophetic mediation between God and humanity. Metaphorical or not, disability's representational role has ramifications far beyond reference to people with various impairments.

*A Communicative Schematic*

An act of communication involves several parties. Hebrew prophecy structures the communication act as a joint operation of God, the prophet, and the audience that the prophet addresses. Overholt's social dynamic model of prophecy includes these basic elements, along with several feedback loops and the appearance of followers.[27] To understand disability imagery in prophetic literature, one must first grasp this dynamic quality of prophecy. Disability imagery both models a "wrong" feedback loop, and also provides additional evidence in favor of a social-dynamic model. Further, the prophet's rhetoric often indicates the presence of a fourth party who has been ignored by the audience—the poor, the powerless (widows, orphans), and yes, the actual disabled—and whose exclusion is one item on the prophetic indictment. Communication can be achieved or disrupted between any pair of these parties. Accordingly, the language of disability can be used to characterize any disruption (it is not used to represent "right" communication). In the prophetic corpus, and more specifically in Isaiah, images of disability fall into four major categories: (1) with reference to the implied audience, disability signifies a refusal of encounter with human others and divine commands; (2) with reference to God, disability can be chosen in order to shut off communication; (3) with reference to the prophet, disability characterizes his relationship with the audience, almost by contagion from the divinely chosen disability; and (4) with reference to the audience after reconciliation has occurred. Actual disabled persons are missing from this list because prophetic literature rarely uses the terms to refer to them; their appearance is the exception rather than the rule.[28] Each of these items requires further nuance, and none of them exists in isolation from the others. I will delineate each in turn and trace the structure of the relationships among them.

When language of disability is applied to the audience of prophecy, it usually accuses the powerful of inability properly to perceive divine and human others. The prophetic discourse thus contrasts an outward

27. Thomas W. Overholt, *Channels of Prophecy: The Social Dynamics of Prophetic Activity* (Minneapolis: Fortress, 1989), 22–23.
28. Sarah J. Melcher, in "'I Will Lead the Blind by a Road They Do Not Know': Disability in Prophetic Eschatology" (paper presented to the Society of Biblical Literature, November, 2004), treated most of the disability imagery as if it referred to actual disabled persons. More recently, Saul Olyan, in "Disability in Prophetic Utopian Vision" (paper presented to the Society of Biblical Literature, November 19, 2007), offered his own taxonomy of the passages; he treats fewer as literal references than Melcher does, but more than I do.

powerful display with an inner condition of disability or disease. These accusations can range from charges that are probably intended in a literal sense to images of disability and illness that are clearly metaphorical. Yet it is not always important to determine literal or metaphorical uses. The opening speech in Isaiah is one of the most stunning examples of this rhetoric. Just after its opening petition for witnesses, the speech describes the people collectively as wounded (1:5b–6). This striking image plays with the usual concept of a wound as localized in an otherwise healthy body: here, wounds compose the whole body, such that the prophet removes the ordinary (and Normal) assumption of health. The speaker then focuses more narrowly on the priestly cults and festivals, carried out in the absence of justice for widows and orphans (1:17). From this sharpening focus, it becomes clear that "my people" who stand accused here are the religious authority figures, and that the images of sickness refer to them. It is just as clear that this extensive corporate woundedness is not a Deuteronomy-style plague. On the other hand, sometimes the prophetic speaker indicates a self-inflicted impairment, for example, priests and prophets who muddle themselves with drink (28:7–8) and thus cannot walk straight. Even this obvious means of self-impairment, however, can be metaphorical. The passage in Isa 29 depicts behavior as a cause of further disability (29:9); stupid is as stupid does, as Forrest Gump said much later.[29] In short, prophetic rhetoric represents loci of ability and disability: the powerful are able to indulge themselves and to oppress others, but are unable to perceive their own injustices and the divine demands for justice. Isaiah 1 asserts that even animals do better. It also launches its trenchant critique of the powerful with this central metaphor of a completely wounded body, as if this image is the starkest contrast possible to the self-image of the addressees. In all of these passages, the prophet indicts the powerful; they are accused of acting disabled when they could act otherwise. Exceptions to this pattern are rare, but I will address that possibility below.

Why use terms such as "blind," "deaf," and "stupid" for people who are not? The terms used of inappropriately powerful humans are closely linked with a divine choice to become disabled. That is, just as powerful humans have refused to see or hear their oppressed fellows or the divine demands for justice, so God refuses to see or hear them. In Isa 1:15, God flatly says that he will hide his eyes and will not listen to such people. Like some of the Psalms, then, Isaiah represents

---

29. Jer 4:22 also contrasts power to do wrong with inability to understand.

a God who may choose a temporary or selective disability: he will be disabled in relation to a specified group. (This is precisely the possibility that Psalm-speakers beg to avert.)

In the next logical step, the punishment for self-inflicted impairment is divinely afflicted impairment: those who do not see or listen are rendered even more incapable of it. After accusing the audience of selective blindness, deafness, or stupidity, the prophetic response can threaten to make the audience really so. Isaiah contains the classically difficult oracle on this theme (6:9–10), in which God commands the prophet to impair his listeners' minds, eyes, and ears.[30] The prophet's speech itself becomes disabling, the means by which these impairments are effected. The command defies expectations that prophets communicate in order to ward off punishment. In this case, crippled communication *is* the punishment. Since the powerful have appropriated a disability to which they are not entitled, the prophet re-asserts God's entitlement by going one better: the impairment the powerful choose to place between themselves and human other becomes an impairment that God places between God's self and the powerful. Selective disability, blindness or deafness, is thus characteristic of both God and the audience. Both choose to close off perception of weaker parties. In that sense, chosen, selective disability makes the powerful more powerful. Paradoxically, it is a display of ability. However the prophetic rhetoric clearly intends to condemn selective disability by powerful human beings—these charges always appear in indictment passages—and to present divine disability as a just response to injustice. As images, then, deafness and blindness can indicate both justice and injustice, depending on who practices them. Even so, Isaiah still makes selective disability the prerogative of the powerful; the difference is that, for the prophet, only God has this special entitlement.

The unfortunate prophet thus has a contradictory mission: he is placed as the medium of obstructed communication, and must communicate just this rupture. It should come as no surprise, then, that prophetic rhetoric so often combines terms of disability with terms of hyper-acute ability. Cross-culturally, intermediaries show characteristic behaviors that resemble physical or mental illness, but intermediation

---

30. Compare Jer 3:5–7. Whether or not Isa 6 is a call scene—I think it is— Sweeney strongly underlines the element of "preparing the people for judgment" (Marvin A. Sweeney, *Isaiah 1–39, with an Introduction to Prophetic Literature* [Grand Rapids: Eerdmans, 1996], 136). It seems that the preparation phase has already passed at this point, and the oracle enacts the judgment.

is a social role more so than a list of traits.[31] In Isaiah, the paradigmatic passage occurs in the exilic strata. The Suffering Servant Song of Isa 42 draws on several motifs that we have examined already. Verses 1–4 employ Second Isaiah's plant imagery to depict the servant's body as strong but not destructive. A divine speech follows in vv. 5–7. These present a "right" form of walking and stipulate the servant's purpose to be a light-bringer and opener of blind eyes (vv. 6–7). What is the nature of this blindness and this light? The following verses operatively define it: they assert the reality of God and the triviality of idols (פְּסִילִים). The next strophe commands the whole earth to sing (vv. 10–13). After that, the focus returns to the single divine, who contrasts his earlier silence with new, earth-altering speech (vv. 14–15). The light/blindness imagery recurs in v. 16, and more significantly, it has an opposite number: those not included are the idol-worshippers (v. 17). Twice, then, the text contrasts two groups, one formerly blind and now sighted, and one that worships idols. If the blindness is literal, this contrast does not make sense. Rather, it is ironic, for this language reminiscent of Deuteronomic polemic uses blindness to represent the worship of visible, material artifacts.

In the context of divine speech representing human worshippers as either blind or sighted, depending on what they worship, the next strophe uses disability language to represent the servant, whom I take to have a prophetic mediating function.[32] This passage most directly exemplifies this fourth type of disabled representation: disability at the point of mediation, in the communicator himself. Verses 18–19 addresses a group as blind and deaf, in keeping with earlier such indictment-language. The passage then directs their attention to the blind and deaf servant.[33] The use of simile suggests that the servant's blindness and deafness are of another kind: he is not blind and deaf like the addressees, or like actual blind and deaf people, but in some other way. Ironically, v. 20 alludes to Isa 6:9–10, but with crucial differences in the language. The servant does see things, without

---

31. Robert R. Wilson, *Prophecy and Society in Ancient Israel* (Philadelphia: Fortress, 1980), 32–35, 42–44.

32. Jeremiah frequently represents prophecy itself as a kind of disease or disability, not inherently but because of the relational and mediating difficulties. See, e.g., Jer 20:7, and compare Ezek 1–3; Hab 1:2–3.

33. Baltzer says that the language is intended to insult (*Deutero-Isaiah*, 149). I agree that it draws on a significant negative valuation of sensory impairment, yet am troubled by his apparent agreement with this valuation. Once again, disability critiques of standard commentaries are an imperative for future research.

paying too much attention to them, and his ears are "open," that is, receptive, but he does not listen. These qualities are valued, for the next verses comment on the servant's righteousness and teaching (42:21), just before attention returns to the people's abjection. This moment amounts to a lament deploring the circumstances into which the servant goes, and looking toward later vindication (42:23). Thus, sensory impairment as an insult to people who do not receive the divine communication has been ironically appropriated to a righteous mediating figure.

Identification of the servant is not important for my purposes; that he stands as a mediating figure, in a function close to if not identical to the prophetic role, is. To say that this figure makes actual blindness and deafness good things would go too far; to say that he heals these conditions would seriously misread. Instead, we have a fine example of that variable quality sensory impairment takes on in Isaiah: it matters *who* is blind or deaf, and what the figure *does* with his or her blindness and deafness. Blindness and deafness thus draw their local value from relational terms, a value that depends on what kind of communication is held up as the model, and what kind is deplored. We might compare the use of muteness in ch. 42, where the prophet says that he has been mute and will now speak (in parallel to a woman going from pregnancy to labor) (v. 14). The audience of the mute prophet is blind, but the prophet will guide them in the right way (v. 16). The idea of a right way or road is a frequent prophetic image, often (but not here) accompanied by the idea of right walking. In any case, the Isaianic imagery of the prophet or other mediator as blind, deaf, or mute, but in a special way, provides a model for the "right" way to use one's sight, hearing, and speech. To return to the passage in Isa 42, the imagery suggests that some things are not worth attention, and if we ask what those are, in this context, the answer seems to be idols and other sorts of triviality. This discloses the final irony of this passage: intentionally or not, the allusions to Deuteronomic critiques of idols have now described the servant, the key mediator, as if *he* were an idol in a Deuteronomic speech.

This may be the Zen koan of Isaiah: when is a prophet like an idol? Consider the mediator's placement in the communication network. When a passage envisages a dyadic communication scheme—God and the people (or the leaders)—the power dynamic described above occurs. In that context, sensory impairment takes on an intentional and hostile tone, where a powerful party exercises power by deliberate, selective impairment. Even God's punishing impairments have a tit-for-tat quality. When a third party, a mediator, enters the mix, we have two related lines of communication, God–prophet and prophet–people. Situated in the middle, the prophet represents each party to the other. Cross-culturally, mediating figures have to access intermediate and unusual states of consciousness.[34] In general, then, it is not surprising that disability images should be attractive to mediating figures, who often take on social disabilities. With respect to Isaiah, the sensory terms mean that prophetic sensory impairment has more possible values than those of God or of the people, since it can be directed in either of two ways. The "right" prophetic arrangement has been subtly represented in Isa 42: blind and deaf to the mundane, hyper-sensitive to the divine, muteness as a matter of timing. After all, the case of blindness and deafness to the divine and hyper-sensitivity to the mundane goes to the people, usually to leaders; it does not describe a possible prophetic or mediating function.

*Who Undergoes Eschatological Transformation?*
Just as Isa 6 represented prophecy as a block to communication, a message that makes itself unhearable by a particular recipient, Isa 29 provides the prophetic resolution for this interplay of sensory impairments. It also contains one of the key eschatological passages that speak of healing, and thus provides a transition to that issue. The larger context of Isa 28–33 form a unit that was redacted much later than the rest of First Isaiah. Sweeney observes that this material contains numerous allusions backward and forward,[35] such that it gathers much Isaianic imagery and thought into a microcosm. The disability imagery is no exception, for it alludes to earlier material discussed above and finds its own further development in portions of Second Isaiah. In Isa 29, several clear links between the initial and final situations suggest that the healings do not refer to actual deaf and blind persons, but rather continue the use of sensory impairment to represent right and wrong communication. A passage early in Isa 29 uses images of blindness, stupidity, and a staggering gait to accuse leaders of irresponsibility (vv. 9–10). These images immediately precede the first sealed scroll reference (vv. 11–12), thus setting the sealed scroll (a form of prophecy) in the context of sensory impairment. The intermediate section criticizes people who "draw near" in speech (v. 13)

34. Wilson, *Prophecy and Society in Ancient Israel*, 32–35, 42–44.
35. Sweeney, *Isaiah 1–39*, 355. He regards the overall genre as prophetic instruction and most of the material as part of a Josianic edition, with the composition of ch. 33 and final editing occurring in the fifth century B.C.E.

but not in behavior or wisdom. It further accuses this group of incorrectly attributing inability to see or know to God (v. 15). After this critique, we have, "On that day, the deaf shall hear the words of a scroll, and…the eyes of the blind shall see" (v. 18). A plodding literal question turns up the metaphor: do the deaf people only hear a scroll, or do they hear other things too? Blenkinsopp notes that this image of the scroll refers back to the sealed scroll, so this passage indicates receptivity to prophecy, not by actual deaf people (who have appeared quite suddenly if they are literal), but by the same group who could not perceive the scroll or other prophetic messages before.[36] The imagery of leading the blind out of darkness (v. 18b) evokes the Isaianic use of those images to represent idolatry, an association that fits with the indictments of Isa 29:13–16 (only here, the people themselves are the artifacts). The only difficulty is the following verse, which humble and needy people now exult at their God (v. 19). But this too picks up earlier language in the passage. In the opening lament, the prophet addressed the city of Jerusalem as deserving of divine punishment, but humbled after the punishment. The appearance of humbled figures later in the chapter may well be an extension of these images. In that case, the language of disability extends to the restored state of the powerful audience that was attacked, disabled, and then humbled.

Two other passages extend this range to the entire people. In this late stratum of First Isaiah, 32:3–5 describe an ideal future kingdom in which the eyes and ears do not close, and the wise and noble remain wise and noble. This provides further evidence that this portion of material is concerned primarily with the corruption of the powerful, for which sensory and cognitive disability provides the main image. Later, in Second Isaiah, the sighted-blind hearing-deaf images of Isa 6 recur in 43:8. There, the context seems to attribute these states to the nations who bear witness, a very large group. This passage clearly does not refer to actual disabled persons, nor does it refer to healing of a physical condition. Rather, the use of these images as metaphors for communication dynamics should be clear. Indeed, the whole trajectory fits perfectly with the ancient Near Eastern belief that the gods sent sickness and disability, and could heal them; only here, the belief plays out on a corporate and symbolic level. At the very least, the images are polyvalent and cannot be construed simply as promises of

36. Joseph Blenkinsopp, *Isaiah 1–39: A New Translation and Commentary* (New York: Doubleday, 2000), 402–6. He gives more latitude than I do to metaphorical readings of healed deafness and blindness in general.

healing for actual disabled persons. The use of the same language to characterize the powerful or virtually everybody renders it suspect in other contexts, and especially in mixed contexts like Isa 29. After all, it was never the blind and deaf who were accused of being blind and deaf when they should not have been.[37]

In terms of whether healing images are literal or metaphorical, Isa 35 is the one atypical case. Historically, it anticipates the return of exiles to a revivified land.[38] In the context of a bizarre and delightful poetic passage that opens with a blooming desert, Isa 35:3–6 asserts that the blind and deaf will have their organs opened up or unstopped, and the lame shall leap like a deer. Given the immediately preceding context, the images set up a parallelism between the land and the people (not surprising): barren land defies expectations by flowering, and disabled bodies defy expectations by demonstrating abilities. One hears some euphony in all the shouting: the desert shouts (רנן, v. 2), and so do the mute (ותרן, v. 6). Why are deserts and mutes *both* shouting? The third strophe describes a sacred way (v. 8) on which the clean, redeemed walk without threat, and return to Zion. Who are these returnees? The only human figures who have appeared thus far in the poem were the blind, deaf, lame, and mute. Will the eschatological Jerusalem be inhabited entirely by disabled persons who acquired or re-acquired their senses? That would be an interesting world, but it does not seem to be the one represented here. The allusiveness between descriptions of land and people, the excessive presence of the disabled, and the general context of uncanny imagery lead me to view this passage in keeping with the wide range of meaning disability has in Isaiah, rather than narrowly as about healing actual people. Probably they are the same people, more exiled than disabled.

To be sure, Blenkinsopp's comment on Isa 28 that "We do not have to choose between a literal and metaphorical restoration of hearing and vision"[39] applies here too and elsewhere, and he is surely correct that prophetic eschatology saw disability and disease as things that would be (literally) gone in the future age. In my view, the best support for the non-existence of disability in the eschatological future is Isa 32:3–4, which does not refer to healing but to the *continued* health and use of sight and hearing in the new age, a belief fully in keeping with the belief that God was the sole etiology of disease, disability,

---

37. Isa 32:2–3 represent continued sensory endowment as a feature of the righteous age. This passage speaks of continued ability, not healing of disability.

38. Sweeney, *Isaiah 1–39*, 453.

39. Blenkinsopp, *Isaiah*, 409. He views Isa 35 as definitely literal.

and healing.[40] The trouble, I suppose, is not the literal-metaphorical question, but whether one views these images in isolation, as single entries in a catalogue of things God can do, or whether one views them systemically as representations of divine–human communication as Hebrew prophecy saw it. That last phrase is perhaps too general, and Isaiah is highly composite. Nevertheless, images of disability in Isaiah and the prophetic corpus generally are polyvalent and complex. On one level, disability is a staple of prophetic rhetoric, and a very apt one for representation of communication. Within the rhetorical structure, disability per se is not good or bad. God's selective disability is treated as appropriate and just, even as powerful. Likewise, the prophet's mission is treated as extremely valuable both in this hyper-ability (the urgent insight) and in its disabling implications (being wounded and cut off from others). By contrast, the metaphorical blindness and deafness of people who should see and hear is judged and punished. And at least some passages of restored sight and hearing probably refer to that same audience who stood accused. The existence of disability, then, does not inhere in individuals but rather occurs between parties in communication, and the value of disability depends on other factors beyond the disability itself: who has it, whether it is intentional or involuntary, whether the agent's intentioned use of it is acceptable or not, and whether it is a metaphor of an inner condition or a literal image of an outer condition. The movement from metaphors of disability to those of ability (for ability too represents more than itself) thus indicates a shift in the quality of communication, from breach to restoration. Lest I be taken to attribute a positive reading of disability to the biblical text, let me note that this entire rhetorical structure depends on the stigma of disability. Isaiah and other prophetic texts simply do not say very much about actual blind, deaf, lame, or other disabled people. Nor do they show any deep interest in what it is like to regain a sense or ability. Even restoration occurs from the point of view of the able-bodied.

*Historical Stratification*
The analysis above has followed the structural nodes of the communication dynamic. Remarkably, the Isaianic corpus is fairly consistent in its representation of "right" and "wrong" communication. The valences

---

40. In my view, one of the weaknesses of Sarah J. Melcher's article ("With Whom Do the Disabled Associate? Metaphorical Interplay in the Latter Prophets," in *TAB*, 115–29) is that it refers frequently to "God as healer" as a metaphor. It might be that for contemporaries, but the ancients meant this seriously.

of the disability images, however, vary and depend on the relational context. I would now like to step into a historical perspective on the material. The disability imagery appears in the oldest layers dating to Isaiah of Jerusalem in the seventh century. The contexts of the Syro-Ephraimite War and the Assyrian crisis seem to have provided occasions for transferring beliefs about illness and disabilities on to the body politic. Further, it seems that Isaiah's advice was ignored on some occasions; this would engender reflection and comment on failed communication, especially if the prophet believed that dire consequences would follow from such failure. Later, the imminent exile and the exilic period greatly embellish this imagery. War is known to be a major cause of disability, and some of this imagery may have come from the later writers' direct experience, in addition to their existing literary and religious sources. Dislocation is difficult; it feels disabling, and arguably is, in the sense that one cannot function in a destroyed city or in a new one in quite the same way as one did before. I suggest that the events of the exile contributed to the frequency of disability imagery in the later strata of First Isaiah, and that the post-exilic context prompted more frequent resort to healing images. Historical context can explain the emphases and nuances that we find in a given passage. However, the entire thought-complex of God-sent illness or disability and God-sent healing is much older; in itself it provides a complete structure, which in turn becomes, in later contexts, a literary and religious resource for adaptation and irony. Finally, I should note that little if any of this imagery values disability as a neutral variation or a positive contribution to the diversity of human embodiment. It is often complex, yet even then, relies on a bedrock of negative cultural valuations. Otherwise, why project a Normal body as the only kind in the ideal future?

## A Brief Excursus on Disability in Other Prophetic Books

The key passages in Hebrew prophecy that are known for speaking of healing for disabled persons are not about disabled persons, and usually do not speak of healing. Indeed, a lack of reference to mended bodies indicates that the disability terms are doing something other than referring to actual disabled persons. The most obvious cases of non-healing are in Jeremiah, Micah, and Zephaniah. Jeremiah 31:8, 9b makes no reference to healing the blind and the lame, and the parallelism with pregnant and newly delivered women amplifies a motif of impaired movement. Indeed, what leaps out at the contemporary disability theorist is that the road is changed, not the people's bodies. (If anyone wants a proof-text for universal design, here it is.) Micah 4:6–7 comes in a larger context of return of peace, the end of war/punishment, and the restoration of Israel. The lame and outcast image, the scattered people, their return, and their re-population. But ingathering is not healing, nor is healing used as a metaphor for ingathering. Status changes, but lameness apparently does not. Finally, Zeph 3:19–20a is quite similar to Micah, both in the reference to lameness and in what occurs to the lame: ingathering and change of fortune come, to figures who apparently remain lame. These three passages are similar in the use of disability imagery, especially terms of mobility impairment, to represent the scattered people. The implied comparison is of exile to lameness. The remedy for exile does not have anything to do with changing anybody's legs or means of locomotion. I contend that the absence of clear reference to healing, and the presence of various terms for renewed power and fortune, indicate an unsustained metaphor: the author easily shifts from exile-as-disability to return as simply wonderful.

## Disability as Communication Nexus

In Psalms and Isaiah, the representation of disability reaches its most complex level in the Hebrew Bible. The dialogical nature of these books—that they represent speakers addressing other in a communication exchange—makes this complexity possible. Virtually all of these uses assume an underlying negative cultural valuation of disability, and yet show a great willingness to play with it, to move it around, to change its value, to be ironic. The language never quite breaks free of the cultural valuations, but the texts do show a keen awareness of disability as relational rather than as a property of an individual body. Beyond that enjoyable complexity, the disability imagery in Psalms and Isaiah is deeply integrated into the worldview. It is not simply one item in the bag of metaphors, where we may pass easily from the metaphor to its referent, or where one metaphor might do just as well. Instead, disability is constitutive of what many Psalms and the composite Isaiah represent about their most important concern: communicating with God.

Chapter 5

LIMPING ON TWO OPINIONS:
DISABILITY AS CONSTITUTIVE ELEMENT
AND CRITICAL MODE

> I talked of things I did not know,
> Wonders beyond my ken.
>
> — Job 42:3[1]

> We become habituated to anything strange by use and time; but the more
> I frequent myself and know myself, the more my deformity astonishes
> me, and the less I understand myself.
>
> —Montaigne, "Of Cripples"[2]

The representation of disability in Hebrew biblical literature is neither simple nor incidental. Across the genres of literature, disability appears most modestly and literally as an impairment that might restrict a priest's cultic performance and most complexly as the (wrong) medium in which Israel's people relate to their God, and God to them. Sometimes biblical texts are "about" disabled persons in a fairly direct way, although I would argue that they are never only that. More often, the Hebrew Bible employs disabled figures or images to represent something else, something more systemic. In their response to the articles in *This Abled Body*, Mitchell and Snyder note: "Most images of disability function as metaphorical equivalents for other social conflicts. Disability is rarely explored as an experience in its own right; rather, like prosthetics themselves, disabled bodies substitute for inadequacies in the larger social body."[3] With respect to the Hebrew Bible (and the New Testament), this

---

1. Pope's translation, cited above.
2. *The Complete Essays of Montaigne* (trans. Donald M. Frame; Stanford: Stanford University Press, 1958), 787.
3. David Mitchell and Sharon Snyder, "'Jesus Thrown Everything Off Balance': Disability and Redemption in Biblical Literature," in *TAB*, 173–83 (177).

negative observation is beyond serious dispute: the Bible never attempts to represent disabled experiences of the body or disabled subjectivity. When disability terms are clearly literal, as in Leviticus, the representational point of view remains the Normal, and disabled figures appear only as Normal ideology registers them. This brings us to the positive point in Mitchell and Snyder's generalization, that disability represents something else. They point to social conflicts, but my interest lies in how disability terms, figures, and imagery contribute to the Hebrew Bible's representation of God. In a nutshell, God is Normal. Further, biblical interpretation tries mightily to make the text Normal. Below, I shall fill out these links between disability and a few major categories of biblical thought, and then suggest how disability might productively be taken up as a critical mode.

### Disability, Power, Holiness, Election

Disability plays a significant, perhaps even indispensable role in the Hebrew Bible's articulation of God's power and holiness, and Israel's election. The Genesis through-narrative intertwines the concepts of God's power and Israel's election with disabled figures. Nor is disability an incidental thread in this tapestry: God's power depends, for its representation, on the disabled human figures. The recurring motif of the barren woman who bears represents a God with power over the human (female) body, also involves God's self in the propagation of the elected line. The various plays on male blindness and sightedness also serve to make room, so to speak, for the divine, rather than human, selection of the important son. This is not to say that Genesis shows God choosing or favoring disabled persons, but rather that being chosen by God disables precisely because the human bodies must show God to be powerful. Jacob's encounter at the Jabbok is the paradigmatic case of theophany as a disabling occasion, and he limps away glad that he is not dead yet (Gen 32:30).[4] Strangely, perhaps, the near requirement of disability does not mean that these patriarchal and matriarchal figures cannot also be dynamic and active; they are, and there is fruitful work here for critique of Normal interpretive traditions. Nevertheless, the disabled patriarchs and matriarchs, together with some subtle sensory representations, prop up both the plot and the representation of God's power and Israel's

---

4. "Not dead yet" is a contemporary disability rights slogan. It expresses defiance at the overt and subtle social message that one must either "get well" or die. In addition, it consciously defies eugenic attitudes and policies, in all their forms.

election. At the same time, God is represented as the Normal, as the non-disabled, as the power that can act and choose "in spite of" the infirmities of human beings.

In a different way, Isaiah and other prophetic books employ disability in the context of rhetoric to enact a drama of communication gone wrong and restored. The prophets are never narrating one line, and composite Isaiah draws together many narrative lines from its disparate historical strata into a symphony (or cacophony) of mutual reference. For all that, the Isaianic use of disability to represent "wrong" communication also contains a narrative arc, from sensory impairment and ruptured communication to sensory restoration and resumed communication. Very much in keeping with Mitchell and Snyder's observation that narrative-enabling disabled figures must be removed at the end, Isaiah repetitiously envisions a future with no disability. This eschaton easily falls under a Mitchell and Snyder phrase, "dreams of similitude," that is, a fantasy of uniform unchanging bodies that codifies a rejection of the varieties and contingencies of actual human embodiment. Mitchell and Synder directed their narrative prosthesis concept to the representation of characters in fiction. Isaiah does not present disabled characters, but uses disability imagery in a way quite similar to the fictional strategies discussed by these authors. Nor does it matter a great deal if the final erasure is "literal" or "metaphorical," for it represents a Normal world that can only be described by reference to the disabled bodies that it abjects.

With regard to the representation of God's power, the book of Job is hyper-typical and atypical. On one level, it enacts a divine assault on a human body, far more detailed than any depicted elsewhere on an individual, but not in principle alien to the thought-world (cf. Gen 32:24–31; Exod 4:24–26). The frame narrative posits some divine insecurity about Job's motives for worship, which only an extreme exercise of power can discern. Indeed, one can read the book as an exposé of the fractures in the Normal God. Without a Job on which to demonstrate power, how would God's power be demonstrated? God points to the natural world, but where would this be without the human audience to impress? Job's recourse to monster imagery is thus right on point: he recognizes that his own weaker, abject body provides the exercise and definition of divine power, as if it were the same sort of thing as the chaos monsters God eliminated. In these ways, the book is hyper-typical in its representation of a Normal God; the very excess nearly undoes the idea. This brings us to the book's atypical quality, that Job's own self-representation, in defiance of his friends' Normal discourse, is left intact and even acknowledged by God as right speech (Job 42:7). Without quite over-riding the divine monologist, Job manages to achieve a self-representation that God does not over-ride. This possibility for the aesthetic transcendence through self-making oddly parallels God's world-making aesthetic discourse, and in this way, the two figures meet. Yet the occasion for Job's self-representation is extreme physical debilitation: disability contributes essentially to this option as well.

Theological readings might see these disability-supported narratives as examples of God's power and goodness. If we look *at* the text instead of through it, however, we see that disability is pervasive rather than exemplary or occasional, and that it actually represents God's power because the text so explicitly contrasts human "weakness" and divine "power." That human beings are not infinitely powerful should not need saying, but neither does it need the inference of this particular kind of deity. That we can imagine deities or sacred essences of unimaginable power is also not the point. The question is whether these texts link the representation of disability to the representation of God's power, and I argue that they do. What one might call the species endowment—a real statistical norm for bodies of a given species—circumscribes the images by which God's power is represented. God gives children to barren women, but God does not give Isaac wings so that he can fly.[5] Either act arguably demonstrates God's power, and yet such acts are selective. A particular ideological Normal, selected from the range of species possibilities, provides the model for God's power, not the other way around.

Disability also constitutes the concept of God's holiness. However similar the emotional response to what we take to be holy, that response cannot justify hypostatizing the Holy as if it always had the same content. Thus, the content of holiness depends on distinctions among a host of concrete, material things for its definition and aura. In fact, a little reflection on cross-cultural encounters reveals differences in the materiality of how holiness is constituted.[6] In Levitical literature, both human and animal bodies play a role in constructing holiness. By excluding

---

5. Since the tradition imagined humanoid figures with wings, i.e., seraphim (Isa 6), I do not think the notion was beyond the scope of biblical imagination.

6. One does not even have to venture into the cross-cultural. I recall a situation on an American university campus where a Catholic student ministry appointed a gay choir director who wore his GALA pin to Mass. Many found his presence affirming of an inclusive God and community. A few objected, publicly and with such a manifestation of physical distress that their sense of profanation was visible. Thus this individual and his materiality evoked holiness to one group and profaneness to the other; conversely, the choir director's supporters would probably have experienced his exclusion as a profanation, while the opponents would feel his removal as restored holiness.

some bodies as less holy, as profane, or as unclean (three distinct categories), the literature clearly states that some kinds of bodies profane the
sanctuary (Lev 21:23). This claim implies that other kinds of bodies
better model holiness. These approved bodies, which are invariably male
and without visible "blemish," thus represent God as similar. To be sure,
the representation is indirect, since Priestly tradition in particular tries to
avoid anthropomorphism.[7] Here, it is important to imagine the performance of the cult, for direct anthropomorphic attributions in language are
not the only way of representing God. The materiality of the cult, what
was acceptable and what was excluded, itself signifies, and it comes
quite close to representing God with smooth skin, even super-human skin
with no orifices or interfaces with the outside. In short, God is the ideal
boundary, which itself is represented by an idealized image of skin.

Some strata of Isaiah also employ the concept of holiness, as if the
ruptured communication were profaning. For instance, Isa 1:4–6 places
the title Holy One of Israel into contiguity with the body composed
entirely of wounds. Such a body would be at least temporarily profane,
in Priestly terms; here, this wounded body images a state of separation or
rupture. Further, the passages of eschatological healing remove several
of the disabilities that Leviticus lists as blemishes, especially blindness
and lameness (Lev 21:18; cf. Isa 29:18; 35:5; Mic 4:6–7 and Zeph 3:19
[lameness only in the last two]). The inclusion of deafness reflects both
composite Isaiah's concern with communication in auditory-oral form
and also perhaps the development of a more inclusive list of profaning
disabilities.[8] Isaiah's advance on Leviticus,[9] then, is to conceive of disability not just as a static property of individual bodies that therefore
must not cross certain spatial borders, but rather as a dynamic quality
manifested in behavior over time. For Isaiah, holy is as holy does, not as
holy looks. Nevertheless, the transposition into action depends upon the
prior valuations of appearance and of disabilities.

Further, images of disability reach even into the Hebrew Bible's most
abstract existential claims about God. They provide fodder for the anti-
polytheist polemics of Deuteronomy and related strata. Once again, the
use of disability to represent idols as unreal indirectly associates sensory
endowment with existence itself, and in so doing, attributes human senses
to God. As with other strata, the species endowment lurks as an unstated
reference point. God is superlatively sighted, and for Deuteronomy,

7. Knohl, *Sanctuary of Silence*, 128–37.
8. We can see this process in the Qumran scrolls' lists in 1QSa and 1QM, among
others. See Melcher, "Visualizing the Perfect Cult," 67–68.
9. I mean "advance" as a greater complexity in the system, not necessarily as a
temporal development.

superlatively hearing, but God never gets a sense of electromagnetism to help God find out what's happening on Earth. Nor is God's or our lack of an electromagnetic sense (or any similar non-human endowment) ever noted or felt as a lack of power. This example may seem silly, and perhaps less silly ones would suffice. The point is that, in evaluating anthropomorphism and any concept of Normal attached to it, it is not enough simply to look for a lesser degree of body imagery in direct divine attributions. One should consider the totality of what is and is not predicated of God. Anthropomorphism and ableism together lurk in what is *missing* from the representation of God. Disembodied though he may be, the Deuteronomic God (and he is male) speaks. How such a disembodied being could produce speech is perhaps a nit-picking question; I only want to indicate that speech itself is a human bodily ability. Deuteronomy has not evaded the human body in its representation of God, and it has represented him as Normal.

Finally, these representations are not static. The idea of divine–human communication is also central to biblical thought. Once again, biblical authors turn to disability as a contrasting element of wrong communication, by which right communication is defined. Interestingly, disability can be used by or occur in either party. The Psalms show some anxiety about a possibly deaf God, and deploy a rhetoric of abasement to prompt God into response. Isaiah, on the other hand, implies that some parties, under some conditions, ought to be deaf or blind; the valence of the disability is a function of who has it and how the possessor uses it. Deuteronomy also clearly contributes to the communicative thread as well. In fact, in the whole Hebrew Bible, Deuteronomy shows the more insistent and exclusive devotion to a single sense, as if its kind of sensory monolatry can ensure that communication between God and Israel remains open. In its excessive concern with hearing instead of looking, it overlooks that fact that one might listen to more than one voice. Once again, in these genres and books where communication figures prominently, the texts use disability to represent "wrong" communication, and by contrast define, often overtly, Normal divine–human communication.

A caveat may be in order here. I realize that my use of Normal in reference to God may strike many readers as exceedingly wrong-headed, for Normal is exactly what God is not. The conventional theological attributes of omnipotence, omniscience, omnibenevolence, and so on, are not normal, not even close. But recall from the Introduction that Normal is an ideological construct, not our colloquial sense of normal as roughly average or typical. However, these terms are related in that a desired portion of human experience is selected, idealized, and elevated to form the ideologically Normal. It should appear as no coincidence that those selections of human embodiment and experience favored by a given society are also attributed to that society's deity or deities. The Hebrew Bible represents God with the abilities it most values in the human (male) body. It multiplies these, perhaps infinitely, but that fact has no bearing on the source of the images. Far from being on the peripheries of biblical concepts, disability contributes significantly, even essentially, to the Hebrew Bible's central ideas. To show that God is real and holy and powerful, the disabled body is constantly pressed into service as God's opposite number.

## Interpretive Prosthesis

Thus the text employs disability to represent its major concepts. Now I would like to turn to questions of how disability can enter the interpretive process, or already be present there. Topics like this one—the presence of an ignored and devalued group in a scriptural text—now come with certain scholarly expectations. One of these could be called Redeeming the Text. This assumption has appeared in my life in several forms, most uncomfortably at a job interview where I was asked to talk about how various biblical passages could be interpreted in a way that affirmed deafness. The question was posed in such a way that "They can't" was not an option;[10] re-signifying the negative as positive was just our job. To draw once again upon a feminist comparison, I find myself in the same camp with Athalya Brenner, who wrote about women in the Hebrew Bible:

> From my perspective, gender issues in the Hebrew Bible can hardly be redeemed for many feminists. Small consolations can indeed be gleaned from one specific text or another; but, on the whole, the so-called Good Book is a predominantly M document which reflects a deeply rooted conviction in regard to woman's otherness and social inferiority. Its M god is made to present, most of the time and against all odds, that he does not really need F company of F properties. Paradoxically, the fight itself is testimony to its futility. In spite of this small victory, the post-reading sensation I experience focuses on the bitter taste in my mouth. This is my heritage. I am stuck with it. I cannot shake it off. And it hurts.[11]

10.   Sometimes, exegetes in the Deaf community take the position that terms that do not refer to a signing Deaf community do not refer to them, but rather to the physical fact of not hearing. (Kirk Van Gilder, Response to Session on Deafness, SBL Annual Meeting, November 19, 2006.) The hearing world, which does not think of itself as such, is largely unaware of this distinction.
11.   Athalya Brenner, "The Hebrew God and his Female Complements," in Timothy K. Beal and David M. Gunn, *Reading Bibles/Writing Bodies: Identity and the Book* (London: Routledge, 1997), 70.

These small consolations are the most I expect to find with respect to disability. To read positively when this clearly violates what we can know about the text and its world strikes me as a breach of intellectual ethics for the sake of comfort, and in the long run, this is not even comfortable. It would also constitute an effacement of the kind that Mitchell and Snyder observe in literature, for it would efface both the historical representation of disability in the Hebrew Bible, and also the historical experience of disabled persons who have undergone signification by interpreters of this text. There is a point beyond which deploring the past becomes a fruitless indulgence; but this effacement would occur in the present, for which I am partly responsible.

That said, I believe that disability studies can contribute a critical mode to the Bible. There is much more work to be done simply analyzing disability in the Bible and its cognate literatures. Historical reconstruction of disabled lives and social status is already well underway.[12] The standard biblical commentaries often do not give adequate attention to disability in the texts on which they comment, and when they do, fail to take a critical stance toward the text's constructions and attitudes.[13] Beyond that, the history of interpretation should prove a particularly fertile ground for scholarly harvest.[14] I, however, wish to close with a proposal of a different nature. I shall suggest one more fusion of Lennard Davis's disability criticism with Jacques Berlinerblau's secular hermeneutics, a combination that brings some new critical tools and metaphors to some old problems. Before reaching for the heights of theory, however, I begin with one concrete case.

*Going Deaf as an Interpreter*
It is a commonplace that interpretation of any text is a dynamic between the text and the reader, and that both parties are situated in a context. Thus the classic hermeneutic circle demands always that the reader become aware not only of the cultural world of the text, but also of his or her own cultural world as it bears on the task of reading. Our cultural world endows us with a set of assumptions which, like air, we cannot do

12. Hector Avalos's works from the 1990s would fall under this category, as would the work of Mikeal Parsons, Rachel Magdalene, Robert Garland, and Fred Rosner. See the Bibliography for these authors.

13. As I noted in Chapter 2, Gerstenberger's commentary on Leviticus does this, as does Baltzer's on Deutero-Isaiah.

14. Nicole Kelley's work takes on this agenda in late antiquity and its religious traditions. See her contribution to *TAB* ("Deformity and Disability in Greece and Rome," 31 45) and her work cited there.

without, and which, also like air, we tend to ignore. It is, after all, invisible. Often we can more easily see the assumptions of other people and other times, for the clash between theirs and ours draws attention. Thus it has become easy to see the predominantly patriarchal bent of the Bible as an object of study, rather than as the invisible air; we breathe a different atmosphere now. When it comes to disability, however, scholarship still breathes much the same as air as the text itself. The entire history of biblical interpretation, theological and academic, shares an assumption with its text, and shares it so closely as to remain unaware of the assumption's operations in the text and in the interpreter—to wit, that the reader can hear. Nowhere in the Bible (Jewish or Christian) does a deaf presence address the reader, nor are deaf readers as such addressed by the text. Sometimes, deafness and deaf people appear, but always, I contend, under the narration or representation of a hearing author addressing hearing readers. Why does this matter? When deafness comes to awareness as a significant element in reading, it raises basic questions about the act of biblical interpretation, questions which have broad implications for the stance of biblical scholarship.[15]

In order to expose these basic questions, I shall explore a highly specific hermeneutical situation: that of a deaf biblical scholar, namely me. Here are the salient features of my microcosmic hermeneutical circle: I am intellectually committed to empirical inquiry as our best means of knowledge about the Bible and anything else; I teach in central Texas, and most of my students are Christians who believe that the Protestant Christian Bible (some stipulate in King James English) is literally inerrant; I am not a Christian; and I am deaf (a late-deafened adult, in the more precise taxonomy of our subaltern world). This constellation of facts, or standpoints, highlights some well-known features of the biblical text, in such a way as to spur reflection that connects certain dots, rather than simply perceiving them as dots. Here is the well-known dot: the Bible uses deafness as a metaphor for spiritual obtuseness, for those who refuse to hear God or a speaker who claims to speak for God. This central metaphor implies that hearing, as the right way to understand textual authority (or, for Deuteronomy, for denying that the authority is visio-textual) connects events and figures in a coherent way, and not just any coherent way but in that particular meta-narrative on which the Bibles, Jewish and Christian, variously insist. Conversely, deafness is the wrong way to understand textual authority, but what are its assumptions, habits, and results? I shall sketch these out gradually.

15. Davis, *Enforcing Normalcy*, 1–22. One relevant passage was cited above, in the Deuteronomy section of Chapter 2.

A single teaching moment contains all of the essential elements on which I would like to reflect. Early in my teaching career, in fall 2000, I was teaching an introduction to the Hebrew Bible. At the time, I had an instructional assistant who transcribed, by hand, a summary of what the students said to me and to each other, so that I could respond. The process is slow and cumbersome, and does not convey the full content of communication. It is, in the language of the ADA, ineffective communication. Around mid-term, the class was in the unit on prophecy, and I read aloud the passage in Isa 6:9–10. I had translated Isa 6 in my dissertation, for a chapter on prophetic and poetic call scenes. At that time—in Chicago in the late 1990s—I thought this passage exceptional in the prophetic corpus because it is one of a handful that does not invite, but rather refuses, communication. Normally, God sends a prophet to communicate, not to make communication impossible. But why communicate the message that communication will become impossible? The oracle seems inherently paradoxical. That's what I thought, and still do.

However, when I read this to my class, I became aware of another paradox. There I was, a deaf non-Christian academic biblical scholar reading this passage to a group composed mainly of literal-inerrantist Christians, and entirely of hearing people. I felt keenly self-conscious, not in the usual way in which I noticed the influence of my deafness on classroom dynamics, but rather conscious of myself as something signified by the text—and signified as a negative judgment from God. Did some of the students sit there thinking that God stops up the ears of people who do not believe in him, and here was a perfect example? I would never know. (I am not an atheist, but most of my students seem to assume that I am.) In any case, the text's allocation of power does clearly support such an interpretation, even though Isa 6 is one of many prophetic passages in which "deafness" is a term that hearing people use to insult each other.

Not only did I realize how students might apply this passage to me, but I also realized that I had never applied it to myself. By this, I do not mean what a hypothetical punishment interpretation means; I never thought of hearing loss and late-deafness as punishments, much less ones in which God would take an interest. It would be more accurate to say that I had never applied myself—my deaf self—to this and similar passages. For years, I had read and translated passages that use deafness as an image of something else, and rarely something good, as if I did not fall within the range of the term's referents. It never crossed my mind that in using terms such as "deaf" or the negation of "hear," the biblical text signified *me*. My lacuna comes, in part, from the historicist training for which the past is always the default setting for meaning. Also, I used to be a hearing person, another cultural default. Only on reading Isa 6 to that particular audience at that time in my life did I become aware that I read as a hearing person, not as a deaf one. It was high time I stopped.

*Interpretation is to the Bible as Prosthesis is to...*
Lennard Davis views deafness as intimately related to disability, and thus finds it possible to discuss a deaf critical mode as a kind of disability criticism.[16] The Deaf community often distinguishes deafness from disability, viewing itself as a linguistic minority, not a disabled population. It is this distinction with which Davis partly disagrees. Thus, my experiences as a deaf biblical interpreter partake of my own understanding of late-deafness as a disability, something distinct from the Deafworld's experience of the signing community. I tend to elide deafness and disability, but there are differences between late-deafness and other kinds of disabilities, and also differences in employing either concept as a critical mode. With respect to the biblical text, a deaf critical mode (in Davis' sense) and a disabled criticism would have much in common, with the former emphasizing the visual-gestural aspects of text and interpretation, and critiquing audism in texts and interpretive traditions. A more general disability approach takes on the text's claims to superlative ability as the only way to be a human being—or an authoritative text.

Thus, I would like to suggest an understanding of scriptural interpretation that draws on some main features of disability. Recall, from the introduction, Berlinerblau's assertion that the Bible is hermeneutically naïve, that it seems unaware of its polysemy and composite nature and instead insists on univocal reading.[17] From a disability perspective, this insistence on univocal meaning in the presence of copious contradictions, ruptures, and unintended polysemy seem similar to denial of a disability. One overlooks the breaks and the variable performances, and instead focuses on what does work, what does fit. However, we cannot attribute any intentionality, much less denial, to the canon, so we must look for the intentional agents who are available: interpreters. Berlinerblau criticizes the overly unifying interpretive strategies common in biblical studies, and faults them with smoothing over too much that is difficult.[18] He refers to this process as supplementation:

> As a prescription for religious life, biblical texts could not be understood in and of themselves. They needed to be explicated, corrected, internally harmonized, and, where necessary, muted by force. Let us use the term

16. Davis, *Enforcing Normalcy*, 1–22.
17. See above, 20.
18. Berlinerblau, *Secular Bible*, 76–77.

"supplementation" as a catch -all category for the process by which early
Jewish and Christian exegetes made sense of Scripture by supplementing
it with texts of their own devising.[19]

But supplementation is precisely the function of a prosthetic. A prosthetic smoothes out, props up, enables a certain kind of functioning (and
sometimes impedes other kinds of functioning). In short, the Bible is
disabled, and much biblical interpretation is a prosthetic performance.

To say that the Bible is disabled is to use a metaphor to describe the
same phenomena that Berlinerblau observes. Yet it is not so much the
ruptures and breaks themselves that make the Bible disabled, but the
combination of these features with its claim to single, clear meaning. On
its behalf, interpreters who extend and sustain this claim to the notion
that the Bible means everything good engage in both prosthesis and
effacement. Even when scholars interpret to the ends of a liberal and
humane religiosity, they partake of the myth of the one right way.
Paradoxically, then, a disability hermeneutic that seeks only the usual
identity-positive re-readings remains a right way of reading, and does not
fully realize disability as a critical mode. Rather than seek affirmation
from the Bible, a disability critique should elaborate the multifarious
ways in which the Bible is disabled, in which others have prosthetized or
passed it, and engage the text's value in terms of the non-omnisemiotic
thing it is. It should ask why anyone needs affirmation from this text for
the specifics of her or his embodiment.

This is not to say that prosthetics are bad things, only that we should
become aware of their prosthetic nature. Prosthesis—I mean, interpretation—cannot over-ride or over-write the nature of the body (text).
Perhaps another autobiographical example can assist with this point. In
2002, I elected cochlear implant surgery. The cochlear implant (CI)
places an electrode array in the inner ear, to replace the function of the
cochlear hair cells that transform mechanical vibrations in a liquid
medium into electrochemical signals in nerves. This array connects to a
computer chip that runs sound-processing software. An external micro-
phone picks up environmental sound, processes it mathematically, and
transmits the digital code as a radio signal to the internal processor,
which commands the electrodes to fire. The brain interprets the result as
sound. Here is the critical question: is a cochlear implant user still deaf?[20]
If one says yes, one effaces the machine and the very real function it

19.  Ibid., 62.
20.  Lennard Davis called this question "the Zen Koan of deafness" in an address
to the MLA-sponsored meeting "Disability Studies and the University," Atlanta,
March 2004.

provides. If one says no, one denies the reality of the body itself, sans machine. CI hearing is not Normal hearing. The Yes-or-No answers to this question both seem wrong. Similarly, if we ask, "Is an interpreted Bible still disabled?" we come to this crux. No: it really does mean such-and-so (women are equal, gay is great, all religions are valuable). This answer employs significant exegetical legerdemain to reach its specific contexts, and effaces the interpretative work, attributes the ability to mean such-and-so to the Bible. Or, Yes: the Bible remains just what it is, and interpretation adds nothing essential. This answer has the virtue of respecting the text's integrity (such as it is), but at the cost of isolating it from the contexts in which it continues to exist and attract attention. It seems to me that liberationist readings efface the text's historicity too much, while fundamentalist interpretation denies that interpretation is occurring and is itself historically conditioned.[21] Not this, not that.

The path forward, I believe, requires refusing the question's dichotomous purity and accepting the impure hybrid that we have. Hybridity applies well to the Hebrew Bible, both in its history of composition and in its history of interpretation. The latter case would be the analogue to human–machine hybrids. An acceptance of the hybrid means a full appreciation of the component parts in their different natures and functions, and an understanding of how these form the composite being. As one final comparison of biblical interpretation to deafness, Berlinerblau's description of historical criticism and even some postmodern biblical interpreters as filling in gaps and smoothing over difficulties in order to retrieve unity from a composite reminds me of the hard-of-hearing strain to construct meaning out of fragmentary audition, visual information on the face, and ingenious guessing from context. That is, biblical scholarship is still too hard-of-hearing. It ought to be hybrid, that is, to embrace the available modes, to stop passing, and to stop prosthetizing. Or to do so only self-consciously, ironically, and *con brio*.

21. Or, "The Bible interprets itself," as one audience member insisted at a forum I organized.

# BIBLIOGRAPHY

Abrams, Judith Z. *Judaism and Disability: Portrayals in Ancient Texts from the Tanach through the Bavli*. Washington, D.C.: Gallaudet University Press, 1998.

Ackerman, Deborah. *A Natural History of the Senses*. New York: Vintage, 1991.

Alter, Robert. *The Art of Biblical Narrative*. New York: Basic, 1981.

Avalos, Hector. *Health Care and the Rise of Christianity*. Peabody, Mass.: Hendrickson, 1999.

————. *Illness and Health Care in the Ancient Near East: The Role of the Temple in Greece, Mesopotamia, and Israel*. Harvard Semitic Monographs 54. Atlanta: Scholars Press, 1995.

Baltzer, Klaus. *Deutero-Isaiah: A Commentary on Isaiah 40–55*. Translated by Margaret Kohl. Edited by Peter Machinist. Minneapolis: Fortress, 2001.

Beal, Timothy K. *Religion and Its Monsters*. New York: Routledge, 2002.

Beal, Timothy K., and David M. Gunn, eds. *Reading Bodies, Writing Bodies: Identity and the Book*. London: Routledge, 1997.

Berlinerblau, Jacques. *The Secular Bible: Why Nonbelievers Must Take Religion Seriously*. Cambridge: Cambridge University Press, 2005.

Biddle, Mark E. "The 'Endangered Ancestress' and Blessing for the Nations." *JBL* 109, vol. 4 (1990): 599–611.

Birch, Bruce. "Impairment as a Condition in Biblical Scholarship." Pages 185–95 in *TAB*.

Blenkinsopp, Joseph. *Isaiah 1–39: A New Translation and Commentary*. New York: Doubleday, 2000.

Brenner, Athalya. "The Hebrew God and his Female Complements." Pages 56–71 in *Reading Bibles/Writing Bodies: Identity and the Book*. Edited by Timothy K. Beal and David M. Gunn. London: Routledge, 1997.

Clifford, Richard J. *Psalms 1–72*. Nashville: Abingdon, 2002.

Coats, George W. *Genesis, with an Introduction to Narrative Literature*. Grand Rapids: Eerdmans, 1983.

Collins, John J. *The Bible After Babel: Historical Criticism in a Postmodern Age*. Grand Rapids: Eerdmans, 2005.

————. *Introduction to the Hebrew Bible*. Minneapolis: Augsburg Fortress, 2004.

Craigie, Peter C. *Psalms 1–50*. Columbia: Thomas Nelson, 2004.

Curtis, John Briggs . "On Job's Response to Yahweh." *JBL* 98 (1979): 497–511.

Davis, Lennard. *Bending Over Backwards: Disability, Dismodernism, and Other Difficult Positions*. New York: New York University Press, 2002.

————, ed. *The Disability Studies Reader*. New York: Routledge, 1997.

————. *Enforcing Normalcy: Disability, Deafness, and the Body*. London: Verso, 1995.

Diewert, David. "Job 7:12." *JBL* 106 (1987): 203–15.
Donne, John. *The Complete Poetry and Selected Prose of John Donne.* Edited by Charles M. Coffin; New York: The Modern Library, 2001.
Dorman, Joanna. *The Blemished Body: Disability and Deformity in the Qumran Scrolls.* Groningen: Rijksuniversiteit, 2007.
Douglas, Mary. *Leviticus as Literature.* Oxford: Oxford University Press, 2000.
―――. *Purity and Danger: An Analysis of the Concepts of Pollution and Taboo.* London: Routledge, 2002.
Driver, S. R. *The Book of Genesis, with Introduction and Notes.* London: Methuen & Co., 1904.
Eisland, Nancy L. *The Disabled God: Toward a Liberation Theology of Disability.* Nashville: Abingdon, 1994.
Fewell, Danna Nolan, and David M. Gunn, "Shifting the Blame: God in the Garden." Pages 16–33 in *Reading Bodies, Writing Bodies: Identity and the Book.* Edited by Timothy K. Beal and David M. Gunn. London: Routledge, 1997.
Garland, Robert. *The Eye of the Beholder: Deformity and Disability in the Graeco Roman World.* Ithaca, N.Y.: Cornell University Press, 1995.
Garland Thomson, Rosemarie. *Extraordinary Bodies: Figuring Physical Disability in American Culture and Literature.* New York: Columbia University Press, 1997.
Gensha (traditionally assigned to). "Gensha on the Three Invalids." Iin D. T. Suzuki, *Manual of Zen Buddhism.* New York: Grove, 1960.
Gerstenberger, Erhard S. *Leviticus: A Commentary.* Louisville: Westminster John Knox, 1996.
Gillmayr-Bucher, Susanne . "Body Images in the Psalms." *Journal for the Study of the Old Testament* 28, no. 3 (2004): 301–21.
Goffman, Erving. *Stigma: Notes on the Management of Spoiled Identity.* New York: Simon & Schuster, 1963.
Good, Edwin M. *In Turns of Tempest: A Reading of Job with a Translation.* Stanford: Stanford University Press, 1990.
Gordis, Robert. *The Book of God and Man: A Study of Job.* Chicago: University of Chicago Press, 1965.
―――. *The Book of Job: Commentary, New Translation, and Special Studies.* New York: Jewish Theological Seminary of America, 1978.
Gruber, Mayer I. *Rashi's Commentary on Psalms.* Leiden: Brill, 2004.
Habel, Norman. *The Book of Job: A Commentary.* Philadelphia: Westminster, 1985.
Hayes, John H. *An Introduction to Old Testament Study.* Nashville: Abingdon, 1979.
Hodgson, Robert Jr. "Holiness." *Anchor Bible Dictionary*, vol. 3, 237–48.
Holden, Lynn. *Forms of Deformity.* Sheffield: Sheffield Academic Press, 1991.
Houtenville, Andrew J. "Disability Statistics in the United States." Ithaca, N.Y.: Cornell University Rehabilitation Research and Training Center. Online: www. disabilitystatistics.org (posted May 15, 2003).
Hull, John M. *In the Beginning, There Was Darkness: A Blind Person's Conversations with the Bible.* Harrisburg, Penn.: Trinity Press International, 2001.
Hume, David. *An Enquiry concerning Human Understanding.* Edited by Tom L. Beauchamp; Oxford: Oxford University Press, 1999.

146 Biblical Corpora

Janzen, J. G. "Another Look at God's Watch Over Job (7:12)." *JBL* 108 (1989): 109–16.

———. *Job*. Atlanta: John Knox, 1985.

Kaminsky, Joel. "Humor and the Theology of Hope: Isaac as Humorous Figure." *Interpretation* 54 (October 2000): 363–75.

Knohl, Israel. *The Sanctuary of Silence: The Priestly Torah and the Holiness School*. Winona Lake, Ind.: Eisenbrauns, 2007.

Kraus, Hans-Joachim. *Psalms 1–59*. Translated by Hilton C. Oswald. Minneapolis: Fortress, 1993.

Lane, Harlan L., Robert Hoffmeister, and Ben Bahan. *Journey Into the DeafWorld*. San Diego: Dawnsign, 1996.

Lindstrom, Frederik. *Suffering and Sin: Interpretations of Illness in the Individual Complaint Psalms*. Stockholm: Almqvist & Wiksell, 1994.

Lohfink, Norbert. "'I am Yahweh, your Physician' (Exodus 15:26): God, Society and Human Health in a Postexilic Revision of the Pentateuch (Exod. 15:2b, 26)." Pages 35–95 in *Theology of the Pentateuch: Themes of the Priestly Narrative and Deuteronomy*. Translated by Linda M. Maloney. Minneapolis: Fortress, 1994.

Longmore, Paul, and Lauri Umansky. *The New Disability History: American Perspectives*. New York: New York University Press, 2001.

Magdalene, Rachel. "The Ancient Near Eastern Origins of Impairment as Theological Disability and the Book of Job." *Perspectives in Religious Studies*. 34, no. 1 (2007): 23–60.

Mandolfo, Carleen. *God in the Dock: Dialogic Tension in Psalms of Lament*. Sheffield: Sheffield Academic Press, 2002.

Marx, Tzvi C. *Disability in Jewish Law*. New York: Routledge, 2002.

Mayes, A. D. H. "Deuteronomy 4 and the Literary Criticism of Deuteronomy." Pages 195–224 in *A Song of Power and the Power of Song*. Edited by Duane L. Christensen. Winona Lake: Eisenbrauns, 1993.

McGuire, Meredith. "Religion and the Body: Rematerializing the Human Body in the Social Sciences of Religion." *Journal for the Scientific Study of Religion* (1990): 283–96.

Melcher, Sarah J. "'I Will Lead the Blind by a Road They Do Not Know': Disability in Prophetic Eschatology." Paper presented to the Society of Biblical Literature, November, 2004.

———. "Visualizing the Perfect Cult: The Priestly Rationale for Exclusion." Pages 55–72 in *Human Disability and the Service of God: Reassessing Religious Practice*. Edited by Nancy L. Eiesland and Don E. Saliers. Nashville: Abingdon, 1998.

Milgrom, Jacob. *Leviticus 1–16*. New York: Doubleday, 1991.

———. *Leviticus 17–22*. New York: Doubleday, 2000.

Mitchell, David T., and Sharon L. Snyder. "'Jesus Thrown Everything Off Balance': Disability and Redemption in Biblical Literature." Pages 173–83 in *TAB*.

———. *Narrative Prosthesis: Disability and the Dependencies of Discourse*. Ann Arbor: The University of Michigan Press, 2000.

Mitchell, W. J. T. "Representation." Pages 11–22 in *Critical Terms for Literary Study*. Edited by Frank Lentricchia and Thomas McLaughlin. 2d ed. Chicago: University of Chicago Press, 1995.

Murphy, Roland. *The Tree of Life: An Exploration of Biblical Wisdom Literature*. 3d ed. Grand Rapids: Eerdmans, 2002.

Newsom, Carol A. *The Book of Job: A Contest of Moral Imagination*. Oxford University Press, 2003.

Niditch, Susan. *Underdogs and Tricksters: A Prelude to Biblical Folklore*. San Francisco: Harper & Row, 1987.

Noth, Martin. *Leviticus: A Commentary*. Rev. ed. Philadelphia: Westminster, 1977.

Olyan, Saul M. "'Anyone Blind or Lame Shall Not Enter the House': On the Interpretation of Second Samuel 5:8b." *Catholic Biblical Quarterly* 60 (1998): 218–27.

———. "Disability in Prophetic Utopian Vision." Paper presented to the Society of Biblical Literature, November 19, 2007.

———. *Rites and Rank: Hierarchy in Biblical Representations of Cult*. Princeton: Princeton University Press, 2000.

Overholt, Thomas W. *Channels of Prophecy: The Social Dynamics of Prophetic Activity*. Minneapolis: Fortress, 1989.

Padden, Carol, and Tom L. Humphries. *Deaf in America: Voices from a Culture*. Cambridge, Mass.: Harvard University Press, 1990.

Parsons, Mikeal. *Body and Character in Luke and Acts: The Subversion of Physiognomy in Early Christianity*. Grand Rapids: Baker, 2006.

Pope, Marvin. *Job: A New Translation with Introduction and Commentary*. New York: Doubleday, 1965.

Preuss, Julian. *Biblical and Talmudic Medicine*. Translated by Fred Rosner. New York: Sanhedrin, 1978.

Raphael, Rebecca. "Academe Is Silent About Deaf Professors." *The Chronicle of Higher Education: The Chronicle Review* (September 15, 2006), B12–13.

———. "He Who Has Ears to Hear." *Spotlight on Teaching* 20, no. 3 (May 2005): x.

———. "Images of Disability in Hebrew Prophetic Literature." Paper presented to the Central Texas Biblical Studies Seminar, Austin, October 24, 2003.

Rich, Adrienne. "Contradictions: Tracking Poems, XVIII," Page 100 in *Your Native Land, Your Life*. New York: Norton, 1986.

Rosner, Fred. *Encyclopedia of Medicine in the Bible and Talmud*. New Jersey: Jason Aronson, 2000.

Sacks, Oliver. *Seeing Voices: A Journey into the World of the Deaf*. Vintage Books: New York, 2000.

Schipper, Jeremy. *Disability Studies and the Hebrew Bible: Figuring Mephibosheth in the David Story*. New York: T&T Clark International, 2006.

———. "Reconsidering the Imagery of Disability in 2 Samuel 5:8b." *Catholic Biblical Quarterly* 67 (2005): 422–34.

Silvers, Anita, et al. *Disability, Difference, Discrimination: Perspectives on Justice in Bioethics and Public Policy*. New York: Rowman & Littlefield, 1998.

Snyder, Sharon L., Brenda Jo Brueggemann, and Rosemarie Garland Thomson, eds. *Disability Studies: Enabling the Humanities*. New York: The Modern Language Association, 2002.

Speiser, E. A. *Genesis: Introduction, Translation, and Notes*. New York: Doubleday, 1964.

Steiner, George. *No Passion Spent*. New Haven: Yale University Press, 1996.

Stewart, David Tabb. "Deaf and Blind in Leviticus 19:14 and the Emergence of Disability Law." Paper presented at the Society of Biblical Literature, Philadelphia, November 19, 2005.

Stiker, Henri-Jacques. *A History of Disability*. Translated by William Sayers. Ann Arbor: University of Michigan Press, 2000.

Sweeney, Marvin A. *Isaiah 1–39, with an Introduction to Prophetic Literature*. Grand Rapids: Eerdmans, 1996.

Walls, Neal H. "The Origins of the Disabled Body: Disability in Ancient Mesopotamia." Pages 13–30 in *TAB*.

Walsh, George B. *The Varieties of Enchantment: Early Greek Views of the Nature and Function of Poetry*. Chapel Hill: University of North Carolina Press, 1984.

Weinfeld, Moshe. *Deuteronomy 1–11: A New Translation with Commentary*. New York: Doubleday, 1991.

Wendell, Susan. *The Rejected Body: Feminist Philosophical Reflections on Disability*. New York: Routledge, 1996.

Werman, Cana. "The Concept of Holiness and the Requirements of Purity in Second Temple and Tannaic Literature." Pages 163–79 in *Purity and Holiness: The Heritage of Leviticus*. Edited by M. J. H. M. Poorthuis and J. Schwartz. Leiden: Brill, 2000.

Westermann, Claus. *Genesis*. Translated by David E. Green. Edinburgh: T. & T. Clark, 1987.

Wilkinson, John. *The Bible and Healing: A Medical and Theological Commentary*. Grand Rapids: Eerdmans, 1998.

Wilson, Robert R. *Prophecy and Society in Ancient Israel*. Philadelphia: Fortress, 1980.

Wolfers, David. *Deep Things Out of Darkness: The Book of Job, Essays and a New English Translation*. Grand Rapids: Eerdmans, 1995.

Wynn, Kerry. "The Normate Hermeneutic and Interpretations of Disability Within the Yahwistic Narratives." Pages 91–101 in *TAB*.

# INDEXES

## INDEX OF REFERENCES

# INDEX OF AUTHORS